AMATEUR HOUR

AMATEUR HOUR

Motherhood in Essays and Swear Words

—

KIMBERLY HARRINGTON

HARPER PERENNIAL

NEW YORK • LONDON • TORONTO • SYDNEY • NEW DELHI • AUCKLAND

HARPER ● PERENNIAL

Reprinted with permission "If Life Were Like Touch Football" by Julie Cadwallader Staub, from *Face to Face*, Dream Seeker Books, 2010.

HarperCollins books may be purchased for educational, business, or sales promotional use. For information, please email the Special Markets Department at SPsales@harpercollins.com.

FIRST EDITION

Designed by Leydiana Rodriguez

Library of Congress Cataloging-in-Publication Data has been applied for.

ISBN 978-0-06-283874-2 (pbk.)

18 19 20 21 22   LSC   10 9 8 7 6 5 4 3 2 1

For Walker and Hawthorne,
thank you for going away so I could write
about how much I love you.

Contents

VOWS

TIME-OUT

SHOWDOWNS

TIME-OUT

SCHOOLS

TIME-OUT

BODIES

TIME-OUT

FREEDOMS

LAST

FIRST

I Don't Want to Be Dying in Order to Tell You These Things

There is a deadline, always a deadline, for me to do anything and all things. I've gone from someone who organized others to one who is organized by those around me, and my former self condescends to me always, *Oh brother, you're really going to take this to the eleventh hour, aren't you?*

And so I think, dying would be an excellent way to write a book. The ultimate deadline, no extensions. I could skate it quite close, until I realized I had taken things too far—again—and maybe couldn't finish. And I would be so mad at myself, as I always am, when I realize I've chosen pushing my luck over pushing myself.

It's not like I'm the first person to think death is the ultimate and most convincing of all deadlines. Neurosurgeon Paul Kalanithi, professor Randy Pausch, and neurologist and writer Oliver Sacks delivered their final insights their way—a book, a talk, and essays that outlasted them. But I am not a dying man with a doctorate. I do not expect my death to be a bestseller.

But I don't want or need to be dying in order to tell you that when you were born my heart cracked right open. The dark things, the alone and sad things, they all slithered across the operating room floor and disappeared down the drain. I thought of ladybugs, of all things, the first time I held you in my puffy and confused state, afraid to look at my stitches and afraid to admit the body has a purpose other than as a place to hang clothes.

Those ladybugs were a sign.

Everything was a sign back then.

I found an unhatched robin's egg in our yard right around the time I found out you were breech, and the delight at its color and completeness soon dissolved into fear. Was this a sign too? Were you doomed to die inside me?

But you didn't, and later your sister didn't. So now there are two of you, signs be damned.

How easy it is to forget the racing to the hospital to check for heartbeats when before you and between you both there were none. How easy it is to forget that life-shortening worry now that I spend most of my time just wanting you to do your homework. How easy it is to forget there was a me before you both fully occupied all corners of my brain and fingers and guts, pulling and pushing, bruising.

Do I have to be dying to tell you I did my damnedest to figure this thing out, this being-a-mother thing, this being-a-parent thing, this working thing, this being-human thing? I've tried to be better but have oftentimes only been worse. I've expected more of you than I certainly expect of myself, to be kind, to not gossip, to be inclusive, to not swear or fight. I love fighting.

You will be disappointed to learn that parents, and adults in general, do not have all the answers. We do not know as much as we project, walking around in our heads and bodies and bluster like that. That for every inconsistency and misstep, unpaid allowance and canceled vacation, we prove ourselves to be the amateurs we've always known ourselves to be. We are as uncertain as you are, but we can't let you know that. We understand life is finite, but we can't bear to look into your eyes with that knowledge. We are left to outfox our fears and punch above our inadequacies.

I want to tell you—while I am healthy and here—that for all my faults, and they would fill another book entirely, the one I do not have is not loving my children. Not perfectly, not selflessly, but in my own way, the best way I know how. I hope for the rest of your lives you will feel over and over again the love you have been unafraid to reflect back at me, your perfectly imperfect mother.

I have done my best to learn from every hard thing that has crossed my path and every soft thing that has snuggled into my lap. I have done my best to not wish any of it away and to experience all the joy and heartbreak I could hold. I have done my best to write down what is often so hard for me to say with real, spoken words. Without making it into a joke. With sincerity.

I have tried.

And with that, this.

JOBS

Fuck. This. List.

If you are a working parent, the time will come for a daycare artwork reckoning. The rivers of scribbles and oceans of finger paintings. The cotton balls and glitter, macaroni and beans glued to flimsy backing. Artwork assembled by teachers and wranglers, pieces children had only a marginal role in. Their names jotted in the corner or on the back, in someone else's handwriting. Not my kid's. Not mine.

Last weekend the reckoning came for me. Five boxes and three bags stuffed full, a stubborn storage of paper memories moved from one house to the next. I fished out the drawings they did with me, on the weekends or on my weekly work-from-home day. The ones I remember as the beginnings of "real" drawing. From my son, a sad apple and an unimpressed banana. From my daughter, bunnies and scraps full of hearts. I search these first jabs at artistic expression, thinking about how well they represent the people they are now. Emotional storms and animal allegiance.

In the mix were daily daycare notes ("She had a great day and played with her best friend!" "He saw a fire truck outside and ate all his apples!"), preschool field-trip recaps, and informational sheets from the pediatrician's office.

But one piece of paper stopped me cold. The List. I had forgotten all about The List. Seven or eight years ago, back when I was done needing it, I must've thought this was something I had treasured and would want to see again. Maybe it'd make me laugh, or bring me back to a specific time I had long since forgotten. Oh it brought me back all right. And my first thought was,

Fuck.

This.

List.

This was my morning out-the-door checklist that I had crafted for my return to work after my second maternity leave. It was everything I needed to have on, near, or with me as I busted out the door each morning. My son was a little over two years old and had only begun walking a few months prior. My daughter was three months old and never slept. My thoughts were like butterflies—fleeting, zigzagging, and completely impossible to catch.

So, The List:

- Bottles
- Lunch box (my son's)
- Breast pump (With a sublist of all the necessary parts, because nothing will make you crack like an egg spiked into the sidewalk more than realizing you forgot the one tiny part that makes your pump work.)
- Wallet
- Hat (Mine or his or hers or theirs? I have no idea now.)
- Their tote bags for daycare (full of changes of clothes and nap blankets and diapers)
- My bag (packed with nursing pads and deodorant)
- Makeup
- Phone
- Water
- Lunch (mine)

I'm surprised I didn't condense the entire list into one word: *brain*. Try to remember your brain, lady.

Like a slap in the face, that list brought back everything that was intensely, nauseatingly hard about working more-than-full-time and having two very young children. I was expected to perform well at both and was doing so at neither. I was exhausted, emotional—many nights falling asleep fully clothed as I nursed my daughter at 7:00 p.m.

The job I had returned to was stressful, most of the time unnecessarily so. We reminded ourselves regularly that, hello, we weren't exactly curing cancer but instead creating catalogs, packaging, print campaigns, and posters for sugar-water manufacturers, shoe companies, and makers of diapers, cleaners, headphones, snowboards, and anything and everything you could wear, consume, or want (and many things it turns out, you didn't). Now that I think of it, maybe we were actually *causing* cancer.

Regardless, it was also the job I had worked up to my entire adult life. From my first days as an intern while still in college, through two advertising agencies and three design studios, this was the job I pursued and was succeeding at. I loved working and still do. A worker with a job has always been the sharpest and most cleanly defined part of my identity. While other girls were playing house, I was playing office. Working hard was my thing. Until living hard challenged it to a duel.

After my second maternity leave, I felt hollow and split, trying to blend back into the world I used to know, as if I wasn't still getting used to the way my new clothes grabbed at my hips or were taut at my chest. Or pretending my milk wasn't letting down at the most impossibly boring moment of a meeting that ran too long. *Yes, I always hug my chest like this, so by all means, please continue*. I'd like to think if the men (and let's face it, it's largely men) who create family-leave policy in this country suddenly found themselves back at work with new bodies, rampaging hormones, and a not-small risk of spontaneously ejaculating every time meetings ran long, things would change. (It's not a perfect analogy, I know. They'd probably just schedule more extra-long meetings).

We need to rethink how the return to work should be done. And when it should be done. My workplace was not the enemy, not really. I had a paid twelve-week leave, the best I could reasonably hope for in this country. And I had a private place to pump. But there is no mistaking: the world of work was not created by women for women, because it doesn't work for us. It celebrates the births of our children with flowers in our hospital rooms and a baby gift sent home, but expects us to snap to and be on our game twelve weeks (or less) after delivering another human being into the world. It subtly—and not so subtly—pressures us to get our shit together, be like we were before, and Jesus don't talk about the kid all the damn time.

I don't look back and regret returning to work. Nor do I think I should've stayed home full-time with my kids. That's not what I wanted to do, period. I was fortunate to work from home some of the time. I was fortunate that my husband's employer allowed him to work four days a week so he could spend every Friday with our kids until both of them were in elementary school. I just wish I could've stayed home longer without risking losing my job. I wish I didn't need that list because my brain was such a pile of garbage that I couldn't remember the most basic of items in the morning. And I wish I could've worked less initially. But what I was doing was working fifty to sixty hours a week, right out of the gate. It's impossible to recommend that.

I also wish these conversations—about different choices,

when a choice is even an option — didn't automatically devolve into a pissing match between working mothers and stay-at-home mothers. We can't all stay home. And we can't all work. We don't all *want* to stay home. And we don't all *want* to work. Most women *have* to work. And a select few never will. Let's embrace that your team will never contain all the women on earth. And neither will mine. Let's embrace the idea that people (that includes women!) are different, with different goals, different measures of success, different skills and talents and pain points. We all make different choices. We can't all make the same choice. So let's embrace that and then let's *move the fuck on*.

While I recognize all the work I did back then during those long, hard hours, weeks, months, and years allowed me to have the career I have now, I just look back and wonder — did it really have to be so hard? Did the choices need to be so stark? And did I need the added pressure of having to act like it wasn't the biggest clusterfuck of all time? That I wasn't being ground to dust?

While we're at it, can we please stop making fathers feel guilty for fully taking their meager paternity leaves? Or expect them to check in, be on e-mail, or even work while they're at home with their new baby?

My husband is a carpenter, and you can't work from home as a carpenter, thankfully. I needed all the help I could get, both times, all the time. So when I returned to work and was shuttling layouts and notes home to my coworkers while they were on paternity leave, I felt like a part of the horrible machine. I knew it was wrong. Because if someone had arrived on our doorstep with work for my husband during either one of our leaves, I would've slapped that shit right out of their hands. Leave us alone. Is that too much to ask?

The early days and weeks and months of a family are sacred. That's what I've come to believe all these years later. They aren't easy, not by a long shot. But they should be untouchable. The time should be longer, our focus less fractured. We have the rest of our lives to be pulled in a thousand different directions. Give us this time to heal, to get to know each other. Give us more weeks and, yes, months to create a foundation we can all launch from.

Give us more time. We all want more time. We'll be better for it when we return.

When I was preparing for my second maternity leave, I wanted everything to be as buttoned-up as humanly possible. I made lists upon lists, copying my teams on every little detail, all in an attempt to disaster-proof my three-month absence. An impossible task to be sure, but for my own peace of mind I couldn't start my leave feeling I had left a single detail unmolested. As I entered the homestretch, I had one last meeting with everyone to review projects and provide status updates along with a list of the freelancers I had lined up to cover for me. And, of course, a list of backup freelancers for those freelancers. I was grilled, a lot, and more often by my female coworkers than the men. Sometimes other women will make your life harder than it really needs to be.

After work I put my head in my hands and mumbled to my husband, "I wish one person would be big enough to say, 'Everything will be fine.' Just one."

On what was close to my last day, in what was close to my last meeting, I sat with a designer I had worked closely with and I again rattled off everything I knew — the lists, the next steps, the backups to the backups, just everything I could shake out of my brain before it morphed into a postpartum blob of jelly. He nodded. He didn't seem that concerned. And then, to my amazement and relief, he said exactly what I had wanted to hear all along, "Everything will be fine." If I could've heard that more. If we could all say it more. If we could all show it more, through our actions, with empathy, with patience, and, hey, how about with our policies?

If you're returning to work or preparing for maternity leave or just wondering how this will all shake out for you, let me tell you right now: *Everything will be fine.* You will make it. You will survive.

I just wish survival wasn't where the bar was set. I wish it didn't have to be so hard or the time so short. I wish we weren't made to feel somehow indebted for policies that are among the very worst in the world. I wish this wasn't the best we could do. Because it certainly isn't. Fuck that list.

We deserve better.

Job Description for the Dumbest Job Ever

TITLE
Mother

SUMMARY
This position manages to be of the utmost importance and yet somehow also the least visible and/or respected in the entire organization. You will enjoy a whole bunch of superficial attention and lip service from culture, advertisers, and politicians but will never receive a credible follow-up in the form of a concrete plan for advancement, support, benefits, or retirement. Please note: although you will coordinate, plan, and do almost everything, you should expect to crash face-first into bed every night feeling like you've accomplished basically nothing. Welcome!

KEY RESPONSIBILITIES
You will be responsible for literally everything, including but not limited to:

- Keeping coworkers alive.
- Related to the above, supervision of all possible hazards including: electrical currents, water in all forms (baths, sheets of ice, swimming pools, Slip 'N Slides, lakes, dodgy sprinklers, igloos, et cetera), table corners, dogs that have food-sharing issues, uncut grapes, playground equipment, bees.

- Plan, purchase, and prepare all meals,* including feeding youngest coworker with own breasts. We know.
- Read every book. Provide verbal CliffsNotes version to adult partner who apparently can't read these same books although you know for a fact he's a college graduate because that's where you guys met. You actually studied together. He's capable of reading, processing, and retaining volumes upon volumes of complex information. Nevertheless. Observe verbal CliffsNotes go in one ear and out the other. Expect increasing levels of rage to be continuously offset by the knowledge you are only growing more superior with each book. You'll find more details on this and other resentment-inducing scenarios in our employee handbook under Section 2: "You're the One Who Wanted to Get Married." Suck it up, doll.
- Become unnaturally intrigued by what gets stains out of clothing, trade tips with other moms and hate yourself for it, bookmark stain chat blogs and hate yourself for it, share hot tips (sunlight! vinegar!) with your friends via text and hate yourself for it. Stitch your vagina shut for good; you are no longer a sexual being.
- Exercise more in less time and with greater difficulty than you ever have at any other point in your life. Expect marginal improvement. You can do it! Sort of!
- Prepare to assume the responsibilities of pets your coworkers have begged for and then subsequently abandoned. Steel yourself for spending $95 on a vet appointment for a pet mouse while you have no fewer than nine mousetraps lying in wait in your basement for her cousins. It's a real *Upstairs Downstairs*–type situation.

---

* Possible exclusion of barbecued meats between Memorial Day and Labor Day.

- Schedule and oversee all medical, dental, therapy, school, family, sports, and camp meetings and appointments. Do not miss a single one; the successful functioning of and all future happiness associated with this organization depend on it. No pressure, sweetheart.

- Plan company off-sites/"vacations." Oversee reservations and coordination of overpriced rental minivan, multiple flights that will ultimately not work out, strange babysitters, creepy outdated tours you had a free coupon for, family-friendly restaurants where all human hope goes to die, and other assorted details. Create packing list. Create shopping list. Create list for house sitter. Create list for pet sitter. Create list of reasons why everyone should go on this godforsaken trip without you. Weep.

- Stay on trend but not too on trend, if you know what we mean. Don't look dowdy, but don't look like you're trying to dress like a teenager for God's sake. Wear things that are flattering but not too revealing. Bare shoulders are okay as long as the rest of your arms are fully sheathed. Please stop wearing capri pants; they look terrible on everyone. Fedoras and big floppy hats should be avoided, unless you're actually at the beach and need to shield your delicate aging facial skin from both the sun and passersby. Bottom line: you're culturally irrelevant—embrace it!

- Create budgets for the week, month, year, five years, until death, after death. Hopefully you'll be reincarnated as someone who understands money.

- Prepare to become proficient at smiling through misery; expert level at doling out cheerful phrases that do not at all reflect one's inner monologue, while also appearing to care about what others have to say (example: "I'm doing great!

And you?"); and beginner level at just straight-up lying (improvement in this last area is inevitable over time).

- Relax! Remember self-care is important. In fact, it's the main focus for most white ladies. You should definitely make time for it. After all the other responsibilities are taken care of, of course. Why are you so tired and crabby? Try harder, please.

SUPERVISOR

This position reports to coworkers younger and less qualified than you. They will also have little regard for your personal space; may pull your shirt up in public; slap you on the ass (also in public); wonder aloud why your arms, legs, and/or stomach are so "squishy"; and will not at all listen to your opinions. They may, on occasion, order you around and be clearly unappreciative of your efforts. You're a woman, you should be used to this sort of thing in the workplace by now.

SKILLS AND EXPERIENCE

Nothing will prepare you for this. Not babysitting, not having a dog, and certainly not your childbirth class. Maybe get some sleep or eat chocolate-covered pretzels in your underpants?

SALARY RANGE AND BENEFITS

Should've mentioned it before, but this is actually an unpaid position. Sort of falls into the same category as other bullshit your friends have roped you into by saying something patently false like, "This could be great!" The benefits vary depending on experience, number of coworkers, and whether you have enough money to hire a staff. PS, you should definitely hire a staff. In the first few years the benefits will mostly consist of coworkers not being able to comment on your alcohol consumption in a loud shouting voice in public, since they haven't mastered full sentences yet. In the later years, your benefits will include unpaid vacation, unpaid sick days, unpaid nervous breakdowns but also someone who will bring you your coffee or reading glasses from the next room where you forgot them. You will have frequent access to the full range of your emotions, especially the shouting- and crying-related ones.

TYPE OF EMPLOYMENT

This is a volunteer, unpaid, full-time job. If you have paid employment outside the home, this is still a full-time job. You will have to sort that out for yourself. The primary purpose of this position is to train your coworkers to become more competent, independent, well-adjusted, and successful than you. Don't be afraid to occasionally whisper "Marry for money" to them when no one's around. Who cares? Times change, love is fickle, and working is hard.

HOW WE MEASURE SUCCESS

Success in this position—while prematurely announced by those who are currently breastfeeding five-year-olds—may only be accurately measured roughly ten or twenty or thirty years after your last coworker has left his or her in-house position. Why are you crying? Please note: once your coworker has moved on, you will no longer be allowed into the majority of his or her waking moments and certainly not the sleeping ones. Your former coworkers will typically not be terribly vocal about whether they feel your tenure was a success, or what they're doing now on a day-to-day basis. Sometimes they won't even tell you what they've had to eat or who they are with! Honestly the feedback process and yearly reviews for this position are a nightmare, if they happen at all. Many employees find Thanksgiving to be an unusually popular time for performance reviews, but we do not recommend it.

SUMMARY

The primary purpose of this position is to train the people you love most in this world to leave you. Forever.

Told you it was dumb.

The Super Bowl of Interruptions

Consider, if you will, the Super Bowl. When you combine fighter jets, a sport that's become the bloated host for an entire country's parasitic soul, and a spectacle that renders parody redundant, you can bet your backside that advertisers will come running just to throw garbage bags full of cash at it. And where garbage bags full of cash are, so are advertising agencies. And where there are advertising agencies and garbage bags full of cash, there are copywriters and art directors willing to cut each other's throats to get a piece of that action.

Creatives are a special breed, some finding themselves in advertising purely by chance, laziness, or a sweet hookup. We are the potential novelists, the frustrated painters, the delusional screenwriters, the weekend illustrators, and the gullible *Mad Men*—or, worse, *Melrose Place*—viewers. On one hand we feel above it all, while on the other we're perpetually at the ready to lose our ever-loving shit over the shape of a color swatch in a product description. We regularly pull a muscle carefully cultivating a sense of cool; a studied casualness of *Hey, man, whatever.*

In reality we are almost never "whatever" about anything. We are right down there, in the petty weeds. We are either seething with insecurity or have so overcompensated for some perceived slight ten years ago that our egos need their own assistant and a wheelbarrow. We have followed a career path founded on never knowing the right answers, and if that's not a recipe for crazy I'm not sure what is. If you work in accounting, there are facts. When you work in a creative industry, you are staking your professional satisfaction on subjectivity. Your fortunes rise and fall on whether someone is "feeling" what you're doing.

Nowhere are all these realities more blatantly on display than in the run up to the Super Bowl. You can know nothing at all about advertising and still know that working on a Super Bowl spot is one of the biggest—if not *the* biggest—"gets" in the industry. But those kinds of gigs aren't just handed out at the door. You don't just cruise into your reclaimed-wood cube with industrial metal standing desk on a Tuesday morning and get handed the brief for a bunch of sponsored Instagram posts and, oh yeah, what's this thing again? Oh right, *A SUPER BOWL COMMERCIAL.* Sometimes you're just lucky or (let's hope) damn talented. Or maybe you're just a sociopath with an especially stunning array of tattoos where your soul should be. Or maybe, just maybe, you're the creative director who's gonna go ahead and assign those plums to yourself. We see you, motherfuckers.

As a middle-aged freelancer who lives in Vermont and also happens to be a mother, I had given up any hope of ever working on a Super Bowl spot. Primarily because I'm smart and can understand situations that are crystalline in their clarity. I can't imagine a person with more strikes against her, at the risk of mixing my sports metaphors.

Super Bowl gigs are often kept in-house, so everyone can enjoy watching their coworkers' sense of self-worth get annihilated on the way to the winning idea. And sometimes they're gifted to fancy creatives who work at big, fancy freelance rates, all while having either exactly zero kids or a wife at home taking care of everything while they wank off deep into the night over bloated pickup trucks and glistening fast-food sandwiches.

And then there's me. When I was laid off, I entered a world where my work was molded around mothering instead of the other way around. If you find yourself in a situation like this, it's extraordinarily difficult to go back to the way things were. You have seen the other side; you are dependent on the daily contact and the rhythm of the school bus, the revolving door of field-trip permission slips, this life free of cubicles and Ping-Pong tables. Plus, let's face it, you are exceedingly lazy now. You can't believe how hard you used to work—what was that even all about anyway? You are spoiled by your retiree-like schedule, where you can go to the market at ten o'clock in the morning and call it a day at two thirty in the afternoon. You have proven the theory, once and for all, that "good enough" wins over "die trying."

Because of this mix of parental attachment and feral freelancer entitlement, I've turned down full-time positions I would've happily stabbed someone in the face for fifteen years ago. I've missed out on freelance gigs with some of the best ad agencies and most prominent brands in the world, all because the thought of being away from my kids for a month or three months at a time didn't really do it for me. When you won't drop your life like a hot potato for work, work drops you like a hot potato. Not always and not forever, but obviously people need to know what they're dealing with. If you can't commit for weeks on end, then you're just not for them. Do you know what kind of freelance female creatives are usually for them? The kind who don't have kids.

But here's the funny thing about life, just when you've long ago accepted there are certain experiences you'll never have, that's exactly when those things come roaring in. Sometimes they

come roaring in via your LinkedIn in-box. And if you're thinking, *This is the only time I've ever heard of anything productive
happening on LinkedIn,* I would just like to say, "Me too."

A creative director who got my name from a mutual friend
reached out with a deceptively innocuous note: something about
needing a particular combination of talents for a project and asking about my availability and interest. I have received roughly
fifty messages like this over the past eight years. And the ones
I've fielded from people I don't know personally usually result in
projects with budgets of anywhere from zero to seven dollars. No
thank you.

I hedged my response, as I always do, indicating I would need
to know more—money, client, timing—before I could give a clear
answer on my availability. As for whether I was interested? I'm a
freelancer; I'm always interested.

We hopped on the phone and that's when he dropped three
key details, as I imagine he was gleefully waiting to do:

Super Bowl.

Car client.

A spot targeted at women.

Two days later, I was on a plane to Detroit.

I'm not saying it's a big adjustment to go from working in a
recliner or at your dining room table or sprawled out across your
bed in Vermont with a dog as your only daytime companion to
being in an all-day briefing session for one of the most important
projects of your professional life, but I will say I was throwing
back half tabs of Xanax like they were Tic Tacs.

But then it all comes back to you. You feel giddy over a briefing deck, a thick stack of paper that includes such classics as
the one thing we want to get across, swiped images, and target-
audience slicing and dicing. I grabbed my phone and scrolled
through the list of all the other creatives on this project, landing

on names I recognized. I stared at the cover sheet to the briefing deck again, the words *Super Bowl Spot* practically telescoping off the page, cartoon-style. There were multiple teams in multiple locations all across the country. Creatives there in person, creatives on the phone, creatives who were so important or busy they had to have their own separate briefing sessions. There must have been forty of us. It might as well have been a hundred.

After our one day of meetings, a quick detour to the Henry Ford museum, and an overwhelming trip through John K. King Used & Rare Books, my new partner and I were able to return home—him on the West Coast and me on the East—and work on the entire project remotely. As much as I like working on-site and with actual humans (most actual humans, okay some, maybe a few), being able to throw myself into this huge important project while still being able to see my kids off in the morning and tuck them in at night was both obnoxious and amazing.

But. There it is, *but*: the other thing about having kids around when you work from home is they interrupt. They interrupt a whole lot. Like sharks with fresh blood in the water, they can sense not only that they're being ignored but also that you must have something important at stake. They don't want to professionally destroy you of course, yet are biologically compelled to do so.

I know this. My own mother worked from home. It's not like I can't see it from their perspective, because I absolutely can. Whenever she was on a call—on a phone attached to the wall no less—I would walk under the cord and flip it over and then walk back under the cord and flip it over and do it again and one more time, over and over and over again until I finally came up against her face in my path, phone pressed against her chest and a hiss of, "Will. You. Stop that?"

Because I've worked from home for almost their entire

childhoods, or at least the part they can remember, we've had long-standing rules about work calls:

- Do not interrupt me.
- I will tell you when I'm going to be on a call and approximately how long it will take.
- Do not interrupt me.
- I will go into my bedroom and close the door to make it easier for you to not interrupt me.
- If you interrupt me, you had better be bleeding.
- I can't emphasize enough that blood should be visible.
- Opening the door, shoving a note in my face, and/or pantomiming your questions all still count as interrupting.
- Actual blood.

The pressure on this project picked up immediately. We began calling into full-team creative reviews that could last two or more hours. Spending that much time in an actual meeting is painful. Spending that much time with a phone pressed to your ear is probably covered somewhere in the Geneva convention.

The upside to these epic calls, at least for me, was listening to all the other teams' ideas. Or at least all the ideas I could listen to until they kicked me off. I figured this was not only my first but also likely my last rodeo on the Super Bowl front. I was determined to get everything I could out of the experience. I wanted to hear how other teams presented (did I even know how to present anymore?), how they approached the work and rationalized it (were our ideas any good?), how they reacted to criticism and redirection (am I advocating for our ideas enough? Too much? Gah.).

This wasn't about who "got" the job. We all had the job, whether we were freelancers or full-timers. We were all getting paid to generate, generate, generate. It was about getting as many ideas out there as quickly as possible, cutting the ones that had no hope of working, and diving more deeply into the ones that had promise. Fueled by a cocktail of panic, greed, insecurity, and bragging rights, we were all a perfect match for a sporting event that is the epitome of every one of those things.

Although I was nervous about sharing our work at first, that nervousness quickly dissipated as a couple of teams presented work that was not only bad but also so tone-deaf as to actually be offensive. And there I was, bathing in the dark joy of listening to fellow human beings go down in flames. High school truly never ends.

My partner and I presented our work and then we hung on. We wanted to gauge where we were in this mix and hear what ideas the other teams were mining. Were we on the right track? Was there something we had missed? As I struggled to listen to the next team I could hear my kids—who were ten and twelve and knew better—getting into it three rooms away. Of course they were. I could hear them through a closed door. Of course I could.

I thought what I always think: *They are definitely going to live with another family after this call.*

Suddenly, screaming. Suddenly, yelling. Suddenly, was that crying? It was so high-pitched I couldn't tell which kid it was or if it was even real. They loved doing that whole fake-cry thing with each other, and maybe that was the case this time. I was hoping so hard. But yeah, I don't know, it was pretty loud and slightly hysterical.

I put my phone on mute and kept trying to listen in. That's when I heard the footsteps running down the hall toward my room.

God*damn* it.

My daughter came flying through the door, attempting to

mouth something at me as I closed my eyes, violently shaking my head while waving my one free arm at her. I pointed at the direction of the living room.

"Get out," I mouthed back. *"Get out of here."*

Exasperated she ran back into the kitchen, grabbed a Post-it and quickly jotted a note down in pencil. She screeched back in and thrust the note at me, with a worried look on her face. At this point I could hear my son crying in the other room. The thought *If everyone's okay I'm going to kill them* flashed in my head.

Maybe you're better than me, but I for one cannot read child-drafted notes and concentrate on an intricate forty-friggin'-person conference call at the same time.

I put my index finger up in the international symbol of "Give your mother a goddamn minute," and I tried to listen, unmute, say something on the call like, "Yup, okay, that timeline sounds good," remute, then read the note that said in all caps "HE'S BLEEDING."

It had finally happened.

The day had come.

I left my room, still on the call, and made my way down the hallway to find my son splayed out on the couch surrounded by no fewer than fifty-five bloody tissues.

I mouthed, *"OH MY GOD!"*

She mouthed back at me, *"I TOLD YOU!"*

He looked over at us with Kleenex stuffed up his nose and his face red and puffy from crying. But he also seemed to have calmed down. Given things didn't seem to be at DEFCON Grab-Your-Jacket-We're-Going-to-the-ER, I looked around, did an exaggerated shrug, and slowly backed away and down the hall while still listening to this pileup of a conference call.

My daughter, incredulous, mouthed at me, "What?! *He's bleeding!"*

And I just looked at her and made a few emphatic gestures; I'm not even sure what they were or what they were supposed to mean. Looking back, I think I was just trying to confuse her to buy time.

I was on that call for another thirty minutes. *Thirty. More. Minutes.* As I sat there, trapped, I wondered if my kids had packed up their belongings into old-timey bandannas on sticks and left me for good. As soon as the call was over, I raced out of my room, sliding on my socks Tom Cruise in *Risky Business*–style, exploding apologies.

By that time, the storm was over. The tears had long since dried and so had the blood. Turns out when you're wrestling with your sister on the couch, even though Mom probably wouldn't want you guys doing that, like, at all, sometimes your face is going to meet your sister's cement block of a knee and next thing you know, What's up, Most Important Conference Call of Your Mother's Life?

"You told us never to interrupt you when you're on the phone unless one of us is bleeding! *He was bleeding!*"

I considered the overwhelming and irrefutable evidence and countered with, "I think you guys should be bleeding more than that. Like maybe a level of bleeding you can't control on your own."

Utter silence as they sat there, stunned.

"Are you serious?"

I stand by it.

My partner and I had our work shot down over and over again; almost all of us did. The focus of the work had also changed completely, away from women and toward something else. Something shinier, something futuristic. Women? So last year, so not #trending. But that's how these things go. Work gets killed, directions change, you keep going. None of our ideas made it through to the final. I still don't have a Super Bowl spot to my name.

But for a time I was the coolest mom around, especially to my son, a Patriots fan. I was working on a Super Bowl commercial. And not just for any old thing, but for a car company. An American car company.

Even when we watched the final spot during the Super Bowl and I said, "That's where my commercial *would've* been," it still somehow felt like the biggest thing I had ever done. Because as time goes on, it gets easier and easier to believe in never. When you are not twenty-five, not a man, not living in Brooklyn or Silver Lake or wherever the cool kids are living these days, when you are disappearing from the radar of American culture both at work and at large, it just gets easier to get the message.

Because what are you going to do? You're already tired. And you're asking yourself all the time, Is it worth it? Do I still want to fight this fight? Do I even have any fight left in me? Or do I want to be with my kids and get by and do nothing all that great professionally? But also, why does having kids suddenly make me irrelevant? All these fucking dudes have kids.

You just start to accept there are things that will never happen, things that have passed you by, things you'll never achieve in a million years. You have plenty of evidence to support this line of thought. But then sometimes, out of nowhere, those things come. And you will find yourself doing the most unbelievable things. Like working on something, anything, to do with the Super Bowl. And you will say equally unbelievable things, like telling your children that maybe next time they should bleed just a little bit more.

I Am the One Woman Who Has It All

As an inhabitant of planet Earth, I've heard a lot of talk about "Can women really have it all?" or "You can have it all, just not all at the same time." Well, guess what, everyone? You're wrong! I *do* have it all. Me! I have all of it.

I have two kids *and* the unspoken pressure to act like they don't exist when I'm on a conference call.

I have a professional mandate to know what's happening in pop culture *and* an eleven-year-old who tells me "to stop trying to act so cool."

I have no problem lying about "having a meeting" when I'm with my kids *and* no problem lying to my kids about "needing to work" when I'm on Facebook.

I have flexible morality *and* rigid immaturity.

I have kids who have forced me to do everything in my life with greater efficiency *and* the professional assumption that I'm now less efficient after having kids.

I have the beginnings of an elderly lady stoop *and* the unsightly chin and neck pimples of a fifteen-year-old.

I have decades of professional experience *and* decades of life experience that tell me never to refer to myself as "seasoned."

I have pointless meetings at work *and* at home. Pointlessness is a key component of my brand.

I have male colleagues who tell me I'm not aggressive

enough and I'll never get what I want out of my team *and* female colleagues who tell me I'm too aggressive and I make them sad.

I have the perseverance to pump breast milk eleventy times a day while on a weeklong business trip *and* the denial of expensing the cost of shipping said breast milk home because most women would probably spend a week away from their four-month-old breastfed baby probably that would be pretty likely that it wouldn't be work-related in any way OH MY GOD DO YOU UNDERSTAND HOW VOLATILE I AM RIGHT NOW?

I have righteous anger *and* more righteous anger. In fact, I have so much righteous anger do you think maybe I'm in the Bible?

I have a delusion I'm in the Bible *and* the makings of a quite popular secular martyr. Do you think maybe I'll end up on Oprah's *Super Soul Sunday*?

I have a fantasy I'll end up on *Super Soul Sunday and* the deep knowledge that if I ever met Oprah I would definitely ask her for money, even though that is definitely not in keeping with the tone of *Super Soul Sunday*. Like, at all.

I have breadwinner status *and* lead-parent status. I have so much status.

I have the confidence to speak my mind, asking hard-hitting questions about the project I'm working on *and* the ability to keep my ears from bleeding when a roomful of male clients explain to me what I don't understand about the female target audience.

I have the ability to listen to your rah-rah, pro-family work-culture speech as if I'm hearing a fairy tale for the first time *and* a deep wellspring of cynicism that makes me want to pat you on the head for being so cute with the lying.

I have pizza delivered and more pizza delivered. I have all the pizza.

I have frustration *and* irritation. Actually those are pretty much the same thing.

Hold up.

Wait.

Maybe I didn't understand the question?

Undone

Yellow legal pads are where my lists live. The work list and school list, the house list and project list. Maybe because they're humble and utilitarian, work in paper form. Or maybe I'm subconsciously lulled by their soft yellow, a sly message to slow down—to stop checking off and instead start checking in.

I've been a list maker since I was a kid; that's when it started, I realize now. I never appreciated what I accomplished each day, I only felt frustrated by what was left undone. *Undone* of course being the perfect word for my mental state related to my list-making habit. I am constantly undone by being undone.

Although I now have fortyish years of evidence to the contrary, deep down I must believe that someday I will actually be done. I'll look down and all I'll see is a satisfying patchwork of crisscrosses and highlighter slashes.

There will be nowhere left to drive, nothing to buy or sell, nothing that needs replacing. The dog will have enough food until the end of time, and every appliance we own will be in fine working order. No teeth will need to be cleaned or x-rayed, filled with fillings or slathered in throat-gurgling fluoride glop. Our weight, blood pressure, and general health will be excellent and unchanging (please, please, please). Children will not grow bigger or taller and therefore will never require new sneakers and socks, shirts or jackets. Their books will always be age-appropriate and perfectly challenging. We will never catch a cold. I will not slip on wet leaves in the woods and come crashing down on my ribs like I did that one time; there will be no medical bills. I will not workout or floss, because I am all done.

Maybe normal people use lists as they're meant to be used, as a daily reminder of things that should be taken care of somewhat soon. I don't like to do things that make sense, so I use lists as a way of outlining how theoretically busy I am while also setting myself up for an infinity loop of self-loathing over my failure to get an impossible amount of things done.

I remember when my daughter was a newborn, a miserable, always-screaming-in-my-face newborn, and my son was barely two years old. It was our first summer in our first home and to say there was no time for its upkeep would be like saying Grey Gardens felt a little lived-in.

In our suburban neighborhood, houses were neatly parceled out with small backyards, shrubs were trimmed, and flowers freshly planted. That summer our yard grew wild. Country wild. To keep up the most base level of appearances, my husband would hurriedly run our lawn mower over our patchy front yard. But our backyard grew out of control, tall grass and weeds. Our dogs, also thoroughly neglected that summer, wore a path through the jungle to do what they needed to do. They must've felt like they were always on a great adventure, stalking squirrels and beetles in the outback.

I remember standing in our kitchen, in front of the sink— bouncing my restless, crabby daughter as she struggled against my neck and chest, clobbering me with her tiny, little balled-up fists—while I peered across the street to the neatly manicured lawn of our retired neighbors. Their bright green and patterned grass like Astroturf and cheerful white planter boxes overflowing with red geraniums practically shouted, "What's up, loser?" from across the street. Our neighbors were out there every day, tend-ing, watering, trimming, and weeding. In the fever dream that is the first few weeks with a newborn, I watched them keep up appearances as I bounced and rocked, unshowered, unrested, and usually unfed.

I tried to wrap my head around having that much free time or caring that much about my lawn and flowers. Or going to bed early and waking only once I felt rested. I imagined walking freely around a yard without another human fused to me, what it might feel like to swing both arms or bend over completely without fearing a baby would fall out of some sort of wrap contraption and right on to her head. It's amazing I had been able to do those very things—thoughtlessly and without the proper amount of appreciation—all my life, and now they felt like the equivalent of a space mission.

Although I felt ashamed of our unruly yard, by the end of the summer I felt grateful our neighbors had been right there, smack in my line of sight. Because every time I looked across the street, it reminded me this wouldn't last. Our babies wouldn't always be babies; our kids wouldn't always be kids. For now, our house reflected the messy process of becoming a family of four. We were swamped with chaos and uncertainty that, at its root, somehow felt hopeful. We were saturated with physical closeness, with need. This was no place for to-do lists, because everything we needed to do was always right in front of, on, or next to us.

Over the next couple of years, I realized lengthy to-do lists were a symbol of luxury—of having the time or money to do something, anything, outside the circle of one's immediate needs. The temporary absence of my paper lists were also symbolic of something else that had gone missing—my mental list of things to fix, to make better, to push harder in my own life.

While I'm sure the desire to improve, improve, improve

loomed in me since I was a kid, it really caught fire when I started my career. I mean, obviously. Bosses, tasks, processes, projects, clients, office supplies, coffee, locations, deadlines, politics, career trajectories, bonuses or lack thereof, promotions, annual reviews, coworkers, HR, there is no shortage of things to get on your high horse about. No shortage of things that are inefficient, dumb, and in need of serious improvement.

It was always like a vacation from panic for my husband when I was completely satisfied in a job, because those stretches were few and far between. Anywhere from three months to two years in a job would be followed with three to five years of pissing and moaning, burning out and freaking out. My next move always utterly unpredictable and not always sensible.

One time I had had enough and quit on the spot, with no backup plan, no savings, no nothing. Well, that's not entirely true. I did stop at the store for beer on my way home. When Jon pulled up in front of our teeny-tiny rental house in Sellwood, Oregon, I stood outside on the front porch waiting. He got out of the car, the look on his face reflecting his confusion as to why I was standing there waiting for him to get out of his car.

"I quit my job."

Without missing a beat or uttering a single word, he got back in the car, started it, and drove directly to the store for more beer and cigarettes. He had been with me long enough to know that just because something might prove catastrophic, didn't mean I wouldn't do it anyway.

Our lives—as a couple, as a family—have always been governed by my dissatisfaction implosions. The lists were simply an attempt to supply answers to my endless questions: *Was this my life? What was my next move? Why is this house so small? Is this all there is?* What I'm saying is, I'm both a joy to be married to and a dream to manage.

So when one child arrived and then another, the relief I felt at being released from my desire to upend things over and over again cannot be overstated. In fact, it was a release from being able to plan anything at all. I had lost control, and no list on earth was going to change that. Like a sudden and slick ocean breeze snaking through an overheated cabin, everything cooled down. For the first time since I could remember I didn't constantly wonder, *Well, what's next?* but instead, *How are we all going to get to the end of this day in one piece?* There was no point in jotting down lists targeted at the future, because the future as a concept felt nonexistent. I was able to experience a little something called "being in the moment." Maybe you've heard of it?

It was a relief to no longer focus on myself, even if eating Wheat Thins and Hershey's Miniatures for lunch might have taken that to the extreme. It was refreshing to get out of my own head and submerge myself in someone else's world, try to crack what they needed, even if the inability of an infant and a toddler to communicate those needs drove me mad.

Introspection is necessary, but it's also exhausting. And the desire to improve is admirable, except when it renders you unable to appreciate anything about the life you already have.

I suspected that once my kids were more independent the gears would again creak back into their relentless, familiar rhythm. I would once again start to wonder about my life, my choices, and my work. I would once again begin to think beyond today and into the threatening future. I would return to my search for what wasn't working and what should be fixed. I would go back to looking forward instead of at everything and everyone that was right in front of me.

I wish I could bottle the essence of that summer and those early years, the nowhere-but-here part. If you had told me then that I'd want to retain anything from those crushing minutes, hours, and days I would've thought you were two slices of bread short of a sandwich. But the window into everything being enough, me being enough, was precious and finite. The rest of it can still go—all those fluids and schedules, Cheerios in snack-size bags and cumulative gray-hair-and-wrinkle-causing fatigue. But not worrying about next week or next year because it might as well be a hundred years away? I would spritz it on my wrists like perfume.

Almost eleven years after that summer, I sat at our dining room table, surrounded by my lists. They were back in full force. They populated my desk, my kitchen table, and my mind like litters of rabbits. I was back to feeling perpetually unsatisfied, consistently behind. For every item I checked off, I added two.

Uncharacteristically, I paused. I stopped the chatter that was doing some killer laps in my brain. And I sat there. I gently placed my forehead against the table and allowed myself to feel the full weight of my frustration. I thought about our neighbors that summer my daughter was born. I thought of holding her in the kitchen window; I can still picture the windowsill, although it was a house ago now—two vintage hobnail glass salt cellars sitting side by side. One blue. One clear. A dried dandelion puff and a pinky print of a sand dollar. A tiny glass bottle with a clutch of violets peeking out, the water evaporating.

"This is what life is," I whispered aloud.

This is what life is. We are still in the thick of life, and this is what it looks like. It is lists upon lists. It is work and school, thank-you notes and errands. As long as we own this house, it will include things that are falling down, apart, or off it. The life I chose isn't without its issues; it will always involve things needing to be done. Right up until it doesn't. And as I am needed less, my lists will get shorter. I will no longer need to concern myself with whether my children have proper shoes for the summer or a library card. It will be a list for one.

A week later, my kids had the day off from school, a day I didn't realize they had off. It's a little scheduling menu item I like to call "Working Moms' Surprise!" Usually when I'm working and they're home—especially when I've had little time to mentally brace myself for it—disaster and frustration loom. One crouched on each shoulder, because there are only devils on days like that.

But that day, the low winter sun flickered through our windows and the dog snoozed to the right of my chair. I saw it and felt it. I noticed. My son read on the couch, and my daughter practiced piano, her high, steady voice broadcasting her lack of cynicism, her not-weary-as-the-damn-rest-of-us-ness. I heard it.

As I worked, I continued to listen, headphones off and down at my side for a change. I listened to the humming and piano playing and dog snoring. And all that quiet, stuffed so sneakily into the gaps. At one point they would switch, it would be my son's turn to practice piano and then the sax, then she'd read in his spot. The dog would wake up and need to go for a walk. Soup was for lunch and my first deadline would be met, one kid out the door later that afternoon for play rehearsal and the other undoubtedly hunched over Legos in his room for longer than feels good on his tall, curved, still-growing back.

Just as, inevitably, things would fall apart too. They would fight or get too silly too fast and one of them would end up mad or being slapped or doing the slapping. Someone would get an elbow "accidentally" to the stomach or ear and all hell would break loose. There would be trouble and separation, as always.

But I knew my husband would be home early to jump in, I'd

meet my next deadline, and we would get to the end of that day, no major highs, no major lows, yet it would feel like the greatest gift. To have just a day, one day to feel it unfold. To really see it instead of sprint past it, checking things off as I went.

As I get older and more people are lost to me, I'm beginning to absorb that an uneventful day is a very good day indeed. The doing, the shuffling and shuttling, the eating and sleeping and, yeah, the fighting too. This is life, together.

I listen to the crows caw outside my window and the squirrels remind me there's no rest for the weary. I can hear the dryer in the basement tumbling and why that's comforting I'm not sure, but it is. This is what life is, for now. Still so much to do, still so much left undone.

Dear Stay-at-Home Moms and Working Moms, You're Both Right

For the past eight years I've lived in the middle ground between two categories of mothering. Of course reducing all of mothering to two opposing sides is such an American thing to do, isn't it? To make it a catfight wrapped in an apple pie.

As mothers, we are fed a steady diet of panic-inducing or choice-affirming headlines. We're told just as many studies support staying at home full-time as support mothers working outside the home. We are pitted against one another at every turn, whether it's in culture, in hot takes, or in our own neighborhoods and classrooms. What working mother hasn't been asked to join the other moms for coffee after drop-off and had to answer, "I'd love to, but I actually have to go to *work*"? And what stay-at-home mom hasn't been treated like the daycare backup on snow days because, you know, she's already *at home*?

But the truth is less shrill than the headlines, comment sections, Facebook, and occasional in-person frictions would have us believe. I spent my first five years of motherhood as a full-time working-in-an-office mom. I worked anywhere from thirty-five- to sixty-hour weeks, sometimes more. In my last year of that job my kids were just under three and five years old. I worked longer days than I had before they were born. It was unsustainable and insane.

During one memorable stretch, I was working every weekend,

trying to fit three months of work into two. With the exception of sleeping and eating breakfast, I spent an entire Memorial Day weekend at work; on Saturday pausing to watch the Vermont City Marathon go past our building. I missed fresh air. During those weeks upon weeks, I would go home for dinner and then turn around and go back to the studio until eleven o'clock or sometimes midnight or one in the morning. One night my daughter, three years old, her face framed by curls, marched over to me as I put my coat on to go back to work. Without a word she tugged on my sleeves and tried to unbutton the one button she could reach. She must've thought if I didn't have my coat on then I certainly wouldn't be able to leave. When we come home, we take off our coats, we kick off our boots, we stay awhile.

When I told her I had to go, her eyes welled up with tears. She crumbled. She had had enough of me leaving every night, every weekend, coming home late, leaving early. And so had I. I was giving my entire life over to this place while my daughter cried and tugged, wanting me home. Naturally, she has absolutely no memory of that moment. Suffice it to say, it's branded onto me for life.

I was laid off when the economy crashed, just six months before my oldest child was to start kindergarten. I was fortunate to transition quickly into freelancing, and since then I've had the kind of schedule that allows me to be the one dropping the kids off at school and picking them up, the rare working mother in a pack of stay-at-home moms who are present for the afternoon bell. I can attend morning poetry readings, be there for field trips and performances, or take them to appointments without sacrificing vacation time or having to lie about my whereabouts (something that, for the record, I used to do regularly and without guilt).

I have been a mother double agent, straddling these worlds and passing seamlessly between the two for the past eight years. And it's given me some perspective on how both "sides" get it wrong. And right.

Yes, working mom, you have missed fresh-from-a-nap rosy cheeks and spontaneous smiles. But you have also missed another human crapping straight up your arm. You have missed the shapelessness of time, given your calendar is parceled out into fifteen-minute chunks. But you've also missed the tedious minutes and hours that parenting young children can sometimes (always) entail.

Yes, stay-at-home mom, you have missed jumping in the shower first thing in the morning without a lot of little feet and hands and eyes interrupting or hustling you out, but you have also missed excruciating conference calls where twelve people try to talk all at the same time and then everyone stops talking at the same time and fifty-five minutes later you think, *Someone else is taking care of my baby so I can do* this shit?

Yes, working mom, you have missed a first. I know you have. Every one of us has. Maybe it was your baby rolling over or sitting up or the very worst—taking his first step or full-on walking. It is a gut punch, no question. But along the way you have probably dodged a bullet or two or a half dozen on the colic or the crankiness, the teething or earache front.

Yes, stay-at-home mom, you have missed sitting around with coworkers, shooting the shit or belaboring lunch plans for later that day. Lunch with adults. You have missed stringing your thoughts together and having them stay that way without someone tugging at your shirt or your hand, to come, come now, and do this thing. But you have also missed the mind-numbing tasks, the manufactured chaos, and the never-ending client dinners that have taken you away from your family. You have missed the things that would make you feel better about your decision being the right one.

Or maybe, actually, you haven't. I have seen every mother question her choices. There is working-mom guilt and stay-at-home-mom guilt because there is enough guilt to go around for each and every mother in this country. And that's assuming you even had a choice. I didn't feel I had a choice, as the breadwinner for our family. But I also really liked my job; I was certainly lucky. For so many mothers the choice isn't whether to work but it's how many jobs to get. It's how to keep everyone's heads above water.

I can only speak from my own experience. And what I know is, when I was a working-outside-the-home mother with much more on my plate than I have now, I did a better job of parenting in many ways and a worse job in others. One small thing that stands out to me is how I used to make pancakes almost every Saturday morning. I felt so guilty over how rushed our weekday mornings were, all of us shoveling cereal in our faces with one foot out the door. And now, while I have no fixed schedule and certainly have my weekends free? It takes a sleepover to get me to deal with pancakes. Pancakes. Is there anything easier than pancakes? I'm not sure there is.

And I know since I started working from home I have patted myself on the back for spending so much time in the same room as my kids, while rarely questioning whether I was actually present. Freelancers don't have scheduled workdays or even a scheduled anything. I'm often on my laptop on a Saturday morning, a Friday night, and most afternoons when they get home from school. So is that better than working away from them, where I could often keep work somewhat contained? Debatable, isn't it?

Back then, before leaving on a work trip, I would create some sort of token for my kids. Behind these gestures was a timeless combination of working-mom guilt along with the ol' "Well, if the plane goes down . . . ," because I like to be optimistic like that. Recently I came across a booklet I had made for them before I left for a shoot. I reused old envelopes from our studio's mailroom for the pages and printed out photos of us together, of me separately, and of the places and things I might see. I stayed up late taping it all together and binding it with a ribbon, all so it would be ready to leave on the kitchen counter early the next morning.

As I flipped through it, all these years later, I was stunned at the amount of effort it took to pull this thing together. Especially given I had undoubtedly had a very long day before I got to work on it. I did this at a time when I was getting little sleep, was exponentially stressed, and had almost no time to myself that wasn't work-related. I thought about how I would never do that now, now that I controlled my schedule and could make five books a day if I wanted to.

I was in awe of former me. Not because I did anything perfectly but because I truly didn't see what a great job I was *already* doing. At the time, I felt nothing could make up for my absence. And I also knew that behind these efforts were a raft of apologies: "I'm sorry I'm away from you. I'm sorry I have to make money, even though sometimes what I'm doing is stupid and utterly pointless." But also "I'm sorry that I'm probably really enjoying at least part of it."

Stay-at-home moms, working moms, all moms, we are allowed to be proud of our choices and to question them; sometimes all in the same day. We have all missed things we wished we hadn't and been present for things so soul-deadening it's a miracle we ever get out of this thing alive.

We have all been left so adrift by our society, our culture, and our government when it comes to the first five or six years of a child's life. We are left to sort it out for ourselves, to cobble together our individual plans. No wonder we take all of this so personally.

If you don't believe me, ask yourself the last time parents were shamed for sending their kids off to elementary school. Why would they be? There is a societal and governmental expectation that all children should attend school; that education is necessary for a child's development and that schools play a critical role in any community. School has our support. Imagine if there was a societal and governmental expectation that all children should attend a quality preschool or daycare program? Imagine the freedom and peace of mind it could offer *all* mothers, stay-at-home and working-outside-the-home alike. Imagine.

Instead, we are held hostage by hysterical pronouncements and blood-pressure-spiking headlines.

Have you ever told someone your child is in daycare? It's an awful word; it's a hard one to get out. It's where babies go to die on their first day. That's the only time we hear about those places. I hated telling people my kids were in daycare because there was always a look, *that* look, that said, "I'm sorry you don't love your baby enough to stay home with her." Sometimes I'd get one of those exaggerated jutted-out-bottom-lip numbers that all but said, "Aww, you know that's just wrong, right?"

Or consider the phrase *stay-at-home mom*. Maybe the house as a home base was accurate four decades ago, but I'm pretty sure I spend more time in my house than stay-at-home mothers do. How does it feel introducing yourself at a cocktail party with that title, surrounded by professional whatevers? Americans do like their ambition. And staying at home with young children is the opposite of ambitious, isn't it? Just tell that to a mother who is on hour fourteen with a partner out of town, two kids under three, a dog who just ate half a birthday cake, and bills that need paying. At least when you work outside the home you have the option of actually leaving work.

I have liked this middle ground I've been in. I'm incredibly fortunate to have experienced it. And it has underlined, more than any other experience, how we are our own worst enemies and our very harshest critics. We hold ourselves to intense and impossible standards. We, of course, don't do this alone. Our culture has set the bar so high that it's hidden in a place where we'll never find it. And, conversely, the bar for fathers has been set so low they can easily step over it on the way to the bathroom.

But please believe me when I say we aren't making nearly the amount of life-altering mistakes we think we're making and we are doing an exponentially better job than we can even comprehend. We are in it deep; we are wrong, *and* we are right, regardless of what side we're on. We are human, and we're doing the best we can. Can we not, just for a moment, save a little charity, a smidge of empathy, a bit of softness of the kind we would extend to our kids and extend it, just this once, maybe a bit each day, to ourselves?

TIME-OUT

Just What I Wanted, a Whole Twenty-Four Hours of Recognition Once a Year

What's this? One single solitary day of recognition on an annual basis? Wow, it's like you can read my mind. It's exactly what I wanted for Mother's Day. Back when I was thirteen months pregnant and my crotch felt like an inside-out cheeseburger solely held together by gigantic cotton underpants I thought, *Maybe, just maybe, there could be a whole twenty-four hours of half-assed thanking in this for me.*

And again, when my nipples were cracked and bleeding and I had to remind myself it's "not okay" to think about wanting to "slap my infant daughter to the ground" when she approached my naked vulnerable breasts with her gaping gummy vise grip born of the river Styx, I knew it would all be worthwhile if just once a year I could get a handmade "napkin card" that had been hurriedly scribbled that same morning.

And most recently, as I sat through yet another school team meeting where I had to really commit to not blurting out, "Jesus, kid, JUST LEARN A TRADE," to try to bring all meetings forever to a real and final conclusion, I thought, *If I could just feel mandatorily appreciated for no more than a day and in all likelihood about two and a half hours max, all of these exchanges with incompetent school administrators, humorless hard-ass teachers, and genuinely helpful and lovely people who are having their love*

of working with children slowly drained out of them by the system,
it will all have been worth it.

And here we are.

What day is Mother's Day again? A Sunday? You mean a day
everyone else has off anyway? Of course. Perfect.

So let me see if I've got this straight—you're saying that me,
a mother, will have the same hours of national recognition also
afforded bobbleheads, lumpy rugs, personal-trainer awareness,
spaghetti, one-hit wonders, Baked Alaska, "hole in my bucket,"
cellophane tape, home warranties, "something on a stick," spiral
glazed ham, beer-can appreciation, cabbage, cheese doodles, and
earmuffs?

Someone pinch me.

Next you'll tell me my personal reward for mentally keeping
track of roughly one thousand food dislikes, dentist appointments,
classmate birthday parties, bike helmets, other mothers to avoid,
weather-appropriate footwear, and snacks to bring to school for
whatever the hell they're celebrating this week will be forcing
some kind of garbage smoothie and a charred heel of bread past
my involuntarily pursed lips with a "Mmmmm-mmmm good"
while noticing that the tulip on my breakfast tray bears a striking
resemblance to one of only two tulips the squirrels managed to
not take out GODDAMN IT. And I have to smile because these
photos are definitely going on Facebook? And to not gag over
that smoothie because honestly I think there might be canned
dog food in it? Or not lose my shit—even a little bit—over that
tulip? Wow, this really is some kind of . . . a day . . . isn't it.

Couldn't I just lock my bedroom door from the inside, smash
my phone, and sleep in instead?

No, don't worry, I get it. If I "complain or don't well up with
crocodile tears over the meager/contractually bound efforts of
my family, then I am a selfish monster who should be grateful

to have ever experienced the sublime and life-affirming joys of motherhood that are myriad, ceaseless, and without parallel in the human experience." And if I "dare to gripe even the tiniest bit it must always, always be immediately neutralized with some kind of pat statement like 'But it's all *so* worth it,' said through an unnaturally tight smile and with the dissociative stare of a hostage." Oh, those aren't my words, that's actually page three of the papers I had to sign before they'd release me from the maternity ward.

I'm trying to think what could really put this whole thing right over the top though. Maybe something about a culture that superficially worships at the altar of motherhood while simultaneously not offering any genuine support or respect, just a whole lot of soft-focus commercials, bad jeans, and sexless minivans? Man, that's good. Or maybe that same culture could also simultaneously shame mothers who pay "too much" attention to their kids while also screeching "WHERE WAS THE MOTHER?!" every time a child so much as gets a wayward mayfly right to the eyeball while enjoying more than five seconds of unsupervised outdoor freedom? Or here's another one—maybe businesses could just decide for themselves what sort of maternity leave they feel like offering, because if capitalism has taught us anything, it's that self-serving empathy should always be used as a recruiting tool. A recruiting tool for people who are already pretty rich to begin with. I'd like that last one worked onto a Hallmark card bordered with roses and white doves, please.

Anyway, I want to thank you all for thanking me on this day of required thanking. Now everyone go outside and play so I can throw up this smoothie and clean the kitchen in peace.

"If Mama Ain't Happy, Ain't Nobody Happy": Revised and Expanded

If Mama ain't drinking coffee and it's before 8:00 a.m., ain't nobody need to be talking to her/me.

If Mama ain't getting paid family leave, ain't nobody need to be wondering where she lives because it obviously ain't Sweden.

If Mama ain't called something other than Mama by total strangers, ain't nobody gonna be getting a smile back. Not happening.

If Mama ain't getting mad or sad about something, ain't nobody gotta wonder if she's stuffing it all down because, oh boy, is she.

If Mama ain't making some mistakes, ain't nobody think that's actually true, do they?

If Mama ain't getting some sort of support after this baby is born, ain't nobody gonna be getting a sibling.

If Mama ain't making the same amount of money for the same job as a man, ain't nobody gonna be hearing the end of it, that's for damn sure.

If Mama ain't given some sort of heads-up to throw on a nice dress and some lipstick the night that she's thrown a surprise birthday party, ain't nobody gonna be liking any of the surprises that come next.

If Mama ain't starting a mommy blog, ain't nobody else need to be starting a mommy blog. All full up, ladies!

If Mama ain't fitting into her pants, ain't nobody need to be stating the obvious at least to her face, seriously—use your head on this one, guys.

If Mama ain't got a job outside the home, ain't nobody gotta say something just plain D-U-M-B like, "I'm so happy I returned to work where I CAN USE MY BRAIN AGAIN."

If Mama ain't a stay-at-home mama, ain't nobody gotta say something just plain mean like, "Why did you have kids if you're not gonna raise them?"

If Mama ain't asking you for some parenting advice, ain't no reason to shoot your fool mouth off, INTERNET.

If Mama ain't enjoying every minute, ain't nobody need to ask her why unless they really want to hear the answer(s).

If Mama ain't loading the dishwasher, ain't nobody gotta leave their dishes on the table as if the only passable bridge between these two mysterious places are middle-aged lady hands.

If Mama ain't told you 121 times to pick up your socks, ain't nobody gotta wonder why because chances are she's probably dead.

If Mama ain't yelling and instead is very, very singsongy, ain't nobody getting out of this one alive.

If Mama ain't breastfeeding, ain't nobody's damn business why or why not—zip it.

If Mama ain't having it all, ain't nobody having it all. Seriously, it's not even an actual thing.

If Mama ain't out of ice cream, ain't nobody need to wonder if there's late bedtime tonight; there is not, go to bed now, I have ice cream to eat.

If Mama ain't running for political office, ain't nobody need to worry because she'll still go ahead and fix the world all by herself just like she does every other thing.

If Mama ain't feeling completely fulfilled, heard, relaxed, and respected, ain't nobody . . . HA HA HA, sorry, couldn't even get through that one with a straight face.

VOWS

Tiny Losses

It was a group lunch, a lunch that included my friends and work partners, ex-coworkers and my husband. We would all meet up after my appointment, although no one besides Jon and I would know I had an appointment that day. Not at first anyway.

I anticipated that morning with torturous glee, the kind of glee that comes from secrecy and surprises. I had been told there was no need to come in before the twelfth week, so I waited and ingested vitamins and daydreamed. *This is only the beginning,* I told myself, no need to rush. I marked off the days on the calendar as we inched toward our first milestone as a family. A family! What a phrase! I thought, *This is probably the only time I'll ever be excited to go to a hospital.*

I had taken a pregnancy test and another one. Positive and positive. I had taken one in the doctor's office, positive again. I mean, how pregnant can you get? I felt the effects, the hangover-like effects that even a good nap and an entire box of mac and cheese can't kill. I had felt sleepy and sore and full of questions. Only Jon and I knew I was pregnant. Otherwise I didn't tell another soul. Not a best friend, not my business partners, not even a stranger, which would've been the safest option. I knew the miscarriage statistics by heart, that one in four or one in five pregnancies are lost before the magic twelve-week mark. I rationalized that if something terrible did happen, no one would be the wiser. I was pregnant, then I wasn't; I would go about my life as if I had just had a bad cold. But let's face it, that wasn't going to happen. Even with my naturally pessimistic nature, some part of me believed I'd be firmly on the other side of those statistics. The three out of four, the four out of five. Just before I reached that three-month mark I felt better—measurably, incredibly, joyfully better. Just like the books and websites and articles said I might.

I marveled at how well it was all working out. I felt completely relieved of the soreness and the nausea. I'd be able to eat a meal with my friends without lurching from the variety of smells and meats and sauces. I wouldn't have to keep secrets anymore either, which was exhausting in its own way. It would all be out there, finally.

I hate surprises, but I like surprising people. And a pregnancy is always the best kind of surprise when you're married and in your thirties, and although you weren't ready and you weren't trying, you also weren't *not* trying, these things happen, and holy shit! I thought about how after all that waiting and keeping my mouth shut and acting like I wasn't about to fall asleep or throw up in my purse, I'd finally spring this big announcement at lunch and what would it all mean? I guess we'd hug or squeal and I'd talk about my due date and maybe I'd even share the name I had in mind. Sawyer, whether it was a boy or a girl. Although, I admitted only to myself, it'd be especially fantastic for a girl. Sawyer Hughes. That is a girl who is going places; that is a girl who will bruise hearts and helm companies; that is a girl who will break big stories, own big dogs, and have her own place in the city and maybe another one in the country. Nothing fancy, a cottage of some sort. And that is a girl who will have me in her corner, always.

Or maybe, just maybe, that will be a girl who will never exist. The gel was applied to my belly and the wand worked its way around. It searched. And searched and searched and searched. Because this was my first ultrasound ever, I was just the kind of happy idiot who didn't know anything might be wrong. Besides, today was the day of sharing great news and us all eating lunch together. Nothing bad happens on a group lunch day, does it?

I waited anxiously for the doctor to come in. Let's get a real expert in here who knows what she's doing. Who knows, maybe heartbeats are hard to find. We waited for the right answer.

"I'm so sorry" is what we got instead.

What we finally saw, as she held the wand still, was a small gray jelly bean resting on its side at the bottom of my uterus, like a stone in an empty bucket. Nothing to see here.

We both started to cry.

I was informed of my options; I could wait it out and miscarry naturally, or I could get a D and C. Fuck waiting it out; I want this out of me. What a thing it is, to go about your life carefully for weeks and months, everything in protection of this little life, imagining this little thumbnail of a thing as a boy, as a girl, with wavy hair, with blue eyes, with limbs and thoughts, growing up, getting married. The brain is a fantasy machine and it will spin out entire biographies for a clump of cells you hadn't even confirmed were actually alive. What a thing, to go suddenly from that imagined endless future to straight down into a dark visceral place where you just want your dead baby gone. Out of you. If you're not alive, well, let's just get on with it then.

We were sent to another waiting room, another nurse, to make an appointment. I walked in a fog, my puffy sad face not at all out of place in the infertility clinic. Jesus, was I infertile now? I feel like ob-gyns don't really understand how triggering their practices are; their waiting rooms, their signage, their mix of patients who are at opposite ends of major life experiences. It'd be like having an oncologist who only specializes in people definitely dying of cancer and people who will never get cancer, guaranteed. But please, wait in this room together so you may see your lives in stark relief.

We sat down. This was not happening.

I sent an e-mail to everyone about lunch: I wasn't feeling well and I was so sorry, but even though I organized this whole thing I wouldn't be able to make it. I used an appropriate number of exclamation points. They didn't know what they didn't know. I was just sick, just like I had planned. I just can't make it; I'm so sorry. Throwing up, you know. No one needs that at their lunch, right?! Question mark, exclamation point.

The morning of my D and C we made our sad, slow way to the hospital. This was not what I had planned for that Friday. Earlier that week, Friday was simply one more step forward in our future together, one in a series of neat, predictable steps you took once you were married. From wedding to honeymoon to buffer period to babies. And now we were moving backward. We were going to need to wait to be ready to start all over again. Waiting to be ready to start. This was stupid.

I had never had any kind of procedure before. I never broke an arm or a leg or had the most minor of surgeries. Unless you count having wisdom teeth taken out, which I do not. This was my first hospital bed, my first IV, and don't those hurt like a motherfucker? My first signing of documents legally warning me that I could die due to complications from general anesthesia ("Sounds great right about now, give me the pen"), and my first maneuvering of a complicated bed. What a beautiful room it was, with windows that looked out at the appropriately gray city of Portland, Oregon. *What a beautiful place it would be to have a baby*, I thought. Instead, it felt quiet and awful.

My doctor came in to check on me before the procedure. I had tried hard to keep it together but then she sat on the edge of my bed. Up until that moment she had always been professional and reserved. At every exam she had taken on the role of annual fertility alarm, asking me if we were considering starting a family. She could sense how cavalier I was being, so she always left me with a gentle, "Just don't put it off too long. It will only get more difficult." But in this moment we were on the same side. Sure, I hadn't tried to get pregnant, but that's exactly what I had done. And then I was not. She quietly but directly began, "I had a miscarriage with my first pregnancy. I really do understand how you're feeling right now. But I want you to know, I went on to have two healthy kids. You will get pregnant again." She paused. "This just wasn't the right time."

The thing was, it really wasn't the right time, we had told each other it wasn't the right time. We were broke and only getting more broke by the day. The design studio I was a partner in was tanking, everything was tanking, from the fallout of September 11. We were in massive debt. When I came across a vintage toy Winnebago camper at a yard sale for twenty bucks I bought it as a symbol, of this time in our lives when we were clearly going to end up living IN A VAN DOWN BY THE RIVER. It was a symbol we had nothing, that we actually had less than nothing, that we owed everyone. And it was a symbol of my own idiocy, that even when we were poorer than dirt I'd still spend my last twenty bucks on a toy camper.

My confidence that my partners and I would sashay into the design world and start making money hand over fist led to ridiculous anticipatory spending and no safety nets. And now I was pregnant. Or I had been pregnant. But we would've made it work had the baby stayed. Had we stayed. Everyone always makes it work, don't they?

I couldn't summon my voice, tears slipped across my cheeks, and I nodded my head to indicate I had heard her, that I hoped, that I wanted to believe what she was saying was true. Jon squeezed my hand. I cried harder. And then I was out. And then it was done. And we were back to not being a family again.

That weekend was an unseasonably beautiful one. It was early May in Oregon, a place where we could usually count on the gray skies and rain enveloping us well past the Fourth of July. I parked myself in the sun in our backyard, drinking beer and smoking cigarettes. After being gentle with my body for so long, I now set out to poison it. Fuck you, body.

I wanted to get numb and stay there. It's incredible to realize now there were no iPhones, no social media, no Facebook. Otherwise I would've been numbing myself with those too. Instead, I let the sun beat down on me and allowed a slow imprecise level of drunkenness to take over. I miss how we used to all have to feel our feelings while we were feeling them, alcohol aside. Now I can't get through writing a slightly challenging sentence without a thirty-five-minute distraction-laced journey through at least three social media platforms. Sometimes five.

I tried to read, but everything I picked up would either not hold my interest—and the last thing I needed was my mind to wander—or incite rage. There are mothers everywhere, and pregnancy and relationships and siblings. There are babies. Alive ones.

I can still feel the heat of that sun on my face; I can see our patchy backyard, the one our dogs had thoroughly destroyed through their Kentucky Derby–like treatment of it. When we had first moved in, there were banks of lavender and mint all around our low-slung deck. After a few months, a clutch of hardy sprigs clung on for their lives. The rest turned to hard-packed dirt. The dogs were soaking in the sun too, occasionally rising to sniff at me, then collapse back into their comas. I turned this way and that, having fully surrendered. I didn't know what to do with myself, given that what had been filling me emotionally and physically was now gone. I begged the sun to bake the sadness out of me.

After just a day, and much to my disappointment, I realized I needed to tell people my news. Our news. Trying to process my grief with someone who was also grieving turned out to not be a solid plan. Plus I think there's nothing quite like drunk dialing your friends in the middle of the day with sad news. I called one of my oldest and dearest friends and told her what had happened, the good news that ended up being the bad news. She was healthy and sane and suggested I take care of myself, maybe go for a walk. Or consider yoga once I was up to it and I was like, "Yeah, I think I'll just drink and smoke. Thanks though."

I didn't tell many people, I started small and close. As it should be. I told only women at first, because, of course. None of them were mothers, not yet. But I felt like they would know as much as I knew at that point. They would understand the disappointment, although none of us understood what it meant to be a parent. They would be appropriately sad for me, and I needed some extra hands on the "being sad for me" front. Mine were all filled up.

I napped and drifted. I went to bed early and late. It's strange to have your calendar suddenly wiped clean. That Sunday I woke in the dark, starving. I needed coffee; I needed brain alterations that were decidedly more morning-friendly. I left the house in search of doughnuts at 5:30 a.m. I had lived on the West Coast long enough to know there would be no Dunkin' Donuts every five blocks and, even if there were, no one would care. Poor Dunkin' Donuts. I drove around trying to find any place that was open, finally landing at a supermarket ten miles away. I beelined it for the bakery and filled a waxed paper bag with chocolate-covered doughnuts with sprinkles. The same doughnuts I would always get when I was a kid, after I washed my dad's car on

Saturday mornings and we'd head to the doughnut shop as a reward. I wondered what kind of doughnuts my kids would want. I wondered if I could even have kids. Maybe I couldn't. Maybe that was my one shot.

As I waited in line to check out, a great cosmic joke played out all around me.

Mother's Day. It was fucking Mother's Day. Are you serious?

I guess all that numbing worked, I thought, realizing I had lost track of the days, of the world around me, my calendar no longer having any use. The Xs ceasing to appear. I was bleeding uterine tissue into my pants and had a hangover and a bag of doughnuts, so by all means, pile on. Fuck you, Mylar balloons and garbage roses encased in clear plastic megaphones. Fuck you, the only Mother's Day cards left in this store, awaiting the shittiest kids and husbands of all time, on the morning of this holiday. Fuck you, me, for not retaining enough common sense and/or sobriety to know not to be out in public today. Fuck you, life.

I scurried home as quickly as I could, like a doughnut-loving vampire, the sun finally rising.

"Do not let me leave this house today. At all," I told Jon once he was awake, looking confused. "It's Mother's Day."

I did not think of myself as a mother. The more people I told the more I heard, "You're still a mother, you'll always be a mother." But I didn't believe that. I didn't believe I had a fully formed angel baby in heaven; I didn't think I had experienced motherhood in any sort of real way, in the kinds of ways that would've made me feel comfortable claiming that title. I hadn't had a baby; I had had a lump of dead cells sucked out of me. Sorry, but that ain't motherhood.

We didn't have a ceremony; I never called the baby (was it a baby?) by name. I never whispered to myself when no one was around, "I'm so sorry, Sawyer; I'm sorry we didn't get to meet you." I never did that. At the same time, the name Sawyer was permanently retired from my list. I wasn't looking for a replacement baby to claim it. So to recap: I didn't feel like a mother, but I had been a mother. And I didn't think there had been a baby, but then I didn't want another baby to have my nonbaby's name. Maybe there was a fantastical part of me that believed my imagined future existed, that there was a Sawyer Hughes living the life I had imagined for him or her. I don't know. I just went with how I felt. As a nonmother mother who had lost her nonbaby baby.

Goodbye, Sawyer Hughes. I wonder who you would've been?

That summer slowly unfolded into Opposite Land. Instead of weeks and months of appointments and salads and vitamins and reading e-mails with subject lines like "This is how big your baby is right now!" I watched our design studio sink further into the world of no projects and no money. Jon and I spent hot afternoons lying in a plastic kiddie pool in our backyard drinking beer as I slipped further and further into not giving a fuck about any of it. Nothing felt within my control, nothing was within my control. Might as well live it up while the ship was going down.

And although my heart was black, my brain continued to whir in the background, a hard drive throwing off alarms. That summer kicked off a lifelong sporadic habit of my waking before the sun and just getting up, feeling wide-awake. My brain was telling me to get to it, but never what that "it" was. Regardless, I listened. It was always productive.

Some mornings I would pad into my small office to write or read. And other mornings I would simply make a cup of coffee and appreciate the stillness, which was productive in its own way. One memorable morning I picked blackberries from our backyard as the first rays of warm summer sun shot through the clouds. I brought them to our kitchen sink, breathing in their earthy jammy scent, pulling pancake mix and eggs and milk from cupboard and fridge. Blackberry pancakes for breakfast, ready so early it was like I was fueling up before heading out to milk the cows. Jon woke up, looked gratefully and alarmingly at the stack of pancakes and was like, "What is happening?" Fifteen years later and that one particular expression of my sleeplessness has never repeated itself.

It became apparent that no matter how much I tried to stuff everything down it would find a way to pop back up. In the middle of the night, in the morning, while eating my lunch, after a single sip of beer. It was always there, gurgling under the surface. I would cry at times and at things that made no sense. But that's grief, isn't it? I needed more structure. I needed more life.

I returned to work. I reentered the world at large, the post–Mother's Day world, the back to our regularly scheduled programming world. It took two weeks before I could handle any sort of social gathering; I just hadn't been up to it. Simply going to the Starbucks on the corner was enough of a regular test of my strength—slaloming through strollers and toddlers, pregnant women and attached infants. Ignore them by picking up a magazine and get ready to be punched in the face with celebrity baby bumps and trending diaper bags. Motherhood and babies are everywhere. They are our stability porn.

The days went by. I told more people, if for no other reason than to relieve myself of having to remember who knew and who didn't. The more my supposedly deep, dark secret came out, the more I discovered that apparently having a miscarriage was as common as having the flu. I felt stupid for suffering alone, even for five minutes. And I realized, as with all grief, that the people who step up aren't always the ones you expected to or needed to. Sometimes the people you counted on the most are the same ones who will actually say the most hurtful, unbelievable shit imaginable. Sometimes grief ripples out and takes the living with them. Bon voyage, assholes.

On the flip side of that are the people who played an indelible role in your teenage years or were a coworker at your previous job or a neighbor you had only traded small talk with. They are the people who live on the fringes of your life who, when given the opportunity, will inexplicably rush in to fill the vacuum in your heart. The vacuum left by people you loved and respected who said things like, "You can just get pregnant again" or "It's probably all for the best" or "Your grandmother/father/dog/best friend lived a good, long life." They will fill the vacuum left by people you had counted on to not shit all over your grief.

Firmly in this camp was the first boy I had ever parked with. Eighteen years earlier, there we were, clothes shoved up and down in broad daylight. I remember I had to mentally prepare myself to make out with him. Remember mentally preparing to make out with someone? "Now if he turns his head this way, then which way do I turn my head?" and even still I managed to turn my head the mirror way he turned his head, and is there anything more embarrassing than that? Little did I know then that the urge to get your hot little hands and mouth somewhere on someone else will always triumph over even the greatest humiliation.

We were never boyfriend and girlfriend. We never had any sort of long-term connection or relationship that would've made sense to revisit or continue. We had gone our own ways early on, while we were still in high school—him with the stoner gearhead crowd and me with a crowd made up of single representatives from every other clique, a high school UN. It was a class of sixty-eight kids, for God's sake; it took real effort to cover all the stereotypes. Like this one over here was a National Honor Society nerd and a jock. Or she was a cheerleader and a theater kid. Regardless. He grew up, not unexpectedly, to be the gruffest, most off-roading, no-bullshit, card-carrying NRA member possible, putting us squarely in epic Odd Couple territory.

I don't know why us reconnecting after almost twenty years worked as well as it did. Maybe like any reconnection after that long, it reminds you that you were young. It reminds you that once upon a time you had afternoons free to haul ass on back roads, get half naked with another person, and still make it home in time for a dinner someone else had prepared for you. It reminds you that you didn't have to pay for your electricity or your house, you didn't have to think about getting married or having kids, you didn't have to think about much at all really. So when you look at that other person all those years later, you see all of that. You are on those back roads, and you are in that back seat. You are under the lights of the high school parking lot, and you are at that pizza place. You see each other, the way you used to. You see yourself, when you were fresh, before life started having its way with you.

This man, this boy from my infinite past, was the only person who offered me an out—a free plane ticket home. And I took it. Within a few days I found myself in the town next to my hometown, three thousand miles away from my house and my husband and my life. My real life and my imagined one. We sat in a diner built in the 1940s, the kind of place that opens at 5 a.m. and closes at 2 in the afternoon. I had a newfound respect for places that opened early. We wolfed down butter-soaked toast and bright yellow eggs. Coffee came in sturdy mugs, and it never stopped coming. As if this scene made all the sense in the world, me being there with him. As if this was how things were going to start being okay again. But somehow, starting with that morning, they did.

That night we drank like fish, the thick summer heat settling in that way it does in New England. And I wasn't in my thirties anymore; suddenly I was in high school again. I felt the thrill of all those nights spent aimlessly crawling the spider's web of back roads, listening to "Night Moves" as steam rose from the asphalt after a sudden storm. I felt familiar and protected, like maybe I had my whole life in front of me again. I was surrounded by fireflies and thickets of overgrown trees. I had always thought of summer as being light, but there was a certain heaviness to summers here. I was back to working on mysteries without any clues.

We went skinny-dipping in the lake near his house in the still darkness. I skinny-dipped a lot back then. Yes, he had a girl-friend; no, nothing happened; yes, my husband would know about all of it when I returned. We stayed up until sunrise. I fell asleep on his couch, the sun blasting into my face in between the blinds. I slept until noon and woke with a searing headache, the kind that makes you want to rip your head off and beat yourself to death with it.

I wasn't gone for long, maybe three or four days. But when I returned home to Portland I was better. I can't explain exactly how or why, but I was. I hated returning to the sadness, but I knew I couldn't avoid it forever. And for the first time I felt like I wouldn't feel that sadness forever. I was ready for whatever might be next. I had to be.

Jon and I went to a friend's party, a party for what, I don't even know. I guess back then no one really needed a reason to have a bunch of people over. And I wound up in the kitchen—of course—with two of our only friends who had kids. One of these women, a dear friend of my husband's, had also suffered a mis-carriage. The baby she lost would've been her third child. We soaked in our back-and-forth and our newfound connection, two perspectives from opposite sides of the mothering spectrum. Our experiences simultaneously intermingled and separate, one from the beginning and one from the end.

She was a levelheaded person, an emotionally in-tune person. She was a mother and a wife. She was smart and empathetic. She was not crazy. She was not woo-woo. So when she told me she had seen a psychic at the urging of her sister-in-law, a psychic who had helped her reconnect with her miscarried baby and that it helped her, that she believed that the connection was real, that the psychic was the real deal, I listened. She said to me with the honesty and clarity of a good friend, "I'm telling you, it helped. It really made me feel at peace." I left the party with something I wouldn't have believed when we arrived, a psychic's phone number jotted down in pencil.

I made an appointment. I set off into the outer reaches of southeast Portland. The outer, outer reaches. Her office was located in a building that had the feel of an abandoned concrete bunker. There was no signage, and I had come alone. I couldn't help but wonder, *Was this the last thing I'd ever do?*

I had never been to a therapist or talked to any sort of professional or semiprofessional or even an amateur about my feelings or my life. I wasn't sure how any of this was supposed to work. Being the natural skeptic that I am, I told her very little about my life because, hello, I'm paying you to be a psychic. Figure out what's wrong with me, please, and tell me what's going to happen next. With one exception: I did tell her about my miscarriage. No need to burn good money over unnecessary mind games. I had to tell her why I was there.

It took me a while to settle in to what was happening. The whole situation was simultaneously strange yet hopeful. The more we talked, the more I began to let the strangeness go and instead open up to the possibilities. I started to understand why people who felt desperate reached out to psychics. It was help beyond help. It was help that broke all the rules.

She told me water was a soothing element in my life, I should be seeking out water whenever and wherever I could. Even listening to the sounds of water would work, she said. I had never realized until that moment how central water had been in my life, from Rhode Island beaches to skinny-dipping my way across pools in LA to the lake I had just returned from. Even for me, a terrifically shitty swimmer, it had the power to make me feel like I was home. I cried, not realizing how much I had been forcing myself to feel normal. Worse than normal, like a robot.

The baby had been a boy, she said. Sawyer was a boy. That it had not been the right time for him. Or for us. She said he was happy and safe and that he loved us. She said more about him, from him, but it's now lost to my lack of replaying it.

A couple of months later I returned to her one last time, when I had a serious job offer in Vermont. I was now the type of person who was consulting a psychic over a job offer. I couldn't even stand it.

We didn't want to leave Portland; it was sickening to even think about. We had always imagined building a family there, taking our baby to the Sellwood pool and berry picking with our kids on Sauvie Island. Roller-skating at Oaks Park roller rink and going to the Oregon State Fair even though that thing was awful.

But our financial lives were in ruin, and my design partners had left to work at Nike. I wasn't established enough to freelance, and besides, there was no freelance to get even if I had been. My work world was tanking and something had to give. Everything else that could already give—our plans, our lives, our hopes— already had. The universe was conspiring to spit us out of a place we loved, that's how it felt. It was going to make us so utterly miserable that we'd have no choice.

I told her a little about my job offer and the location. I said I was worried that the job would not only be impossible, that the scope of it seemed crazy, but also that I was more concerned

be a step backward. It was similar to a job I had
and didn't want to do anymore. And although the
...ont was exciting—we had spent time there during
our monthlong road-trip honeymoon and had added it to our list
of places we'd like to live someday, but obviously when we were
retired, because what jobs could there possibly be?—the thought
of leaving Portland and Oregon and the West Coast behind was
the saddest I had felt since losing the baby.

At the end of our session she said, "Your job will be hard,
but it will allow you to do everything you want to do," and she
added, "You will have a boy and a girl there. Everything you've
ever wanted is there."

I left my job; we left Oregon; I sold my '65 Chevy; we left
our friends; we brought our dogs. My job was hard. But in ways
big and small over many years and then due to the absence of it
entirely, it allowed me to do exactly what I wanted to do.

I have a boy.

I have a girl.

I have everything I've ever wanted.

After our first child was born, I put together some photos of
him and wrote a letter to my ob-gyn in Portland. I told her she
was right, it hadn't been the right time then, but it was now. I
told her I was a mother and this cute baby right here? This was
my son. I thanked her for everything. I thanked her for giving me
permission to hope.

If You Love Your Grandparents, Go Visit Them

1. Arrivals

Florida has never been on my list of favorite destinations (sorry, Florida). But since I moved back to New England I've embraced the fact that without Florida, the Winter Ship of Sanity would set sail forever and burst into flames on the horizon.

I'm a searcher and a ground gazer, so from the very first time I saw pictures of the beaches of Sanibel Island strung with thick garlands of carnival-colored shells, I knew I wanted to go. And I wanted to bring my kids, who only knew the hard-won small sand dollars of Maine or the occasional freshwater-snail shell delivered from Lake Champlain. I was hungry for abundance in the dead of winter, for saturated color and steam-soaked air.

When we landed at Fort Myers, I was immediately struck by the formations of grandparents dotting the arrival area — couples, singles, flocks. One with a tentative cane, another with obedient curls, all with the look of permanent tourists. Relaxed, tan, and sporting Florida T-shirts with swoopy beach graphics. Their faces bright with expectation.

I hadn't thought much about my grandparents while planning this trip. I'd never been to Sanibel Island before, and for all I knew, neither had they. I had never connected my memories of my grandparents and their life in Florida with this trip until that very moment. As soon as I did, my heart felt the way a bruise does when it's newly discovered, tender to the touch, a purplish surprise.

I thought of all the times I should've visited them. I thought of all the times it could've been them waiting for me. I thought of all of the trips I could've made happen but didn't.

2. The Rearview Mirror

When I was little we lived in Rhode Island, next door to my maternal grandparents. I rode to nursery school on the back of my grandmother's bike. I played in their garden and plucked the tiniest blue-white flowers from the shaded patch of our mutual yard. And although my family eventually moved to Wisconsin and then to Massachusetts, I spent two weeks out of every summer staying with them, just one block from the beach.

The details, the indelible details, of those days. The way my grandfather rose before the sun, humming to himself and stirring his coffee over and over again. I can still hear the spoon circling around clanging against the inside of the cup, a meditation.

The days were long and free, full of high-stepping-bare-feet-on-searing-asphalt walks to the beach, searching for shells and pulling seahorses from fishermen's nets. My friends and I put on fashion shows and plays in the backyard, pinning a sheet to the clothesline for a theater curtain. We baked cupcakes and I learned how to properly make a bed. I caught tiny jellyfish in a jar and learned how to sew. I ate seedless grapes and a nightly dish of vanilla ice cream and rivers of Cheez-Its. I felt loved and cherished, cared for and fussed over.

I never knew how good I had it. Do any of us, ever?

3. Unforgivable, Merciful Fate

Their early lives were punctured with loss. My grandmother is a first-generation American and one of nine children. Her mother, my Portuguese great-grandmother, was often a single parent, throwing out her husband for the uncontrollable drinking that would eventually kill him.

Her sister Dorothy, who had been institutionalized for reasons we never knew, died at the age of fourteen. Probably from neglect, probably from the way people who were confined to a "school for the feeble-minded" were treated.

There had been a passed-down story about her possibly falling in the tub when she was three or four. Maybe she had suffered some sort of serious brain injury. Then a late-night conversation only a few years ago unearthed a bit of family hearsay—she used to flap her hands. And one of her sisters, now in her nineties, confirmed Dorothy had been institutionalized before she had even turned five. I was thunderstruck. All of these fragmented bits of information, decades old, suddenly collated. She was autistic. She had to be. Autism has threaded itself throughout our family in whispers and shouts. It is seen and unseen. Diagnosed and undiagnosed. It is a part of us. She was a part of us.

Sometimes, when we think we are not moving forward as a society, that progress is not fast enough, that our humanity is utterly lacking—and there are plenty of occasions to think all of those things—we would do well to pause and think of Dorothy. Out of the arms of her mother, away from the eyes of the world. What did they do to her? If she were a child now, how profoundly different would her life be? The powerless and the vulnerable, forever the canaries of our morality.

My grandfather was one of six children and grew up poor in Pennsylvania coal-mining country. Both of his parents died by the time he was seven. His oldest brother, Bill — only seventeen at the time — took on the unfathomable task of keeping his own family together. Bill's girlfriend, Eva, who became his wife, was fifteen maybe sixteen at the most. A teenage girl, an adoptive mother of five. Imagine.

His brother Andy died on the train tracks as he walked home from fishing with his older brother. He was only seven, his brother just eleven. The tracks had switched for an oncoming train, trapping his foot. Immediately bound to his fate, he couldn't be freed. His brother helpless, left to bear witness to the unimaginable. All of the children in the family would grow up to one day warn their own children away from train tracks with a fiery sternness born of heartbreak.

From these dark circumstances, their early lives dotted with absence and need, grief and unforgivable fate, came two of the lightest and most joyful people you could ever hope to meet. Quick to laugh, quick with a hug, and quick to pick up the check (and uncharacteristically upset with you if you tried, as I once learned the hard way). What they had lost early on, they gained in each other. Forever.

Sometimes fate has no mercy. And sometimes it will save you.

4. Big Life

Eventually they went the way of the snowbird — to Florida part-time and then full-time, enjoying the type of retirement that no longer seems to exist. They became a part of a community that cooked, swam, traveled, golfed, sunbathed, played cards, dressed up, and, quite frankly, lived it up more than I ever had.

Whenever I spoke to my grandparents, one on the main phone and the other on the extension, talking over each other, they always gave me the weather report followed by "You know you can always come to Delray!" They invited me to visit every time we spoke. Every time. I always begged off. I knew I would see them when they traveled north to visit. And I didn't have the money or enough time off for an additional trip. But if I had had the money I wouldn't have spent it on a trip to Delray Beach to stay with my grandparents in their retirement community. I have a sharp memory of saying those actual words out loud. Not to them, never to them.

All I knew is that I needed to start my big life and go to big destinations that had bigger and better things for me to do.

Looking back now, I never felt guilty about not going, because they never made me feel guilty about not going. Their lives were bursting there, full. They didn't need me to visit to fill up what was missing. They wanted me to visit because they loved me. Simple.

But was guilt really the reason to go anyway? Who has the big life now?

5. Hello, Goodbye

I've been to Florida maybe five times in my life, all at very different stages of my life — and theirs. I was a twelve-year-old road-tripping with my family from Massachusetts to visit them and hit Disney World and Epcot. I was a twenty-nine-year-old newlywed on a cross-country road-trip honeymoon, where it felt like their entire retirement community had cooked for days just to host a feast for us. And I'm talking some old-school Italian ladies from Rhode Island and New Jersey, so when I say feast, I mean a for-damn-real *feast*. I remember very clearly having to lie down on the floor with my pants unzipped for a good hour to have any hope of making it through dessert. That same night, several of her friends came over to hug me, give me a card or small gift, and wish us a happy married life. One of them looked up at me and then over to her friend and yelled, "Remember when we used to be that tall?!"

On my last visit I was a thirty-eight-year-old mother of two with my eight-month-old daughter in tow. I brought her to meet my grandfather for the first and last time. He loved babies. And he was dying. His eyebrows lifted, ever so slightly, at the sight of her. His animated, head-tilted-back laugh was already gone. But there she was. And so was he. And never would that meeting, those old eyes meeting new, ever happen again.

When I returned to Vermont I spoke to him one last time. I don't remember most of what was said. The call was brief; he would die just a few days later. But toward the end of the call I quietly said, "I should let you go"—as if this was a routine call, as if I could really ever let him go, how bound we are to our conversational shortcuts—"I don't want to tire you out." He replied slowly and with a catch in his voice, "You will never tire me out."

Ten years later, that thought, the intention behind it, the love I felt so crisply and clearly from his weakening voice, still floods me with sadness. I have never let him go.

"You will never tire me out." Isn't that what we all want to hear? To believe?

My grandmother was never the same after he died. Maybe the kind of marriage they had is a thing of the past, I don't know. Born during conventional wartime (if anything about war can be considered conventional) and success that's modest yet inspires generosity, what they had feels almost foreign to this world now. Their marriage wasn't fractured by the simultaneous invented closeness and real distance of technology but bound up in handwritten letters and photographs printed on beefy squares of paper edged in metallic ink. Built to last.

She has survived so much, a brain aneurism and surgery,

breast cancer, strokes. But losing him was the beginning of what continues to be a long, slow, sad end. I've sat in front of her, not being able to grasp the person I once knew. The always ironing, lipstick-mark-from-kissing-you, independent trailblazer of a grandmother I knew my whole life. The one who made her evening gowns and bikinis by hand and the one who taught the neighborhood kids how to bake. And the one who—the last time I visited them in Florida—was rummaging through a basket of photographs, held up a school picture of a child none of us recognized, and said "Who is this kid?" and threw it in the trash. She's lost to most of us now, locked in a place that she sometimes reaches out from, remembering her birthday or tracing invisible dance steps with her fingertips.

My aunt, who lives down the road from my grandmother, visited her last week and noticed she's losing weight. Her wedding band is close to slipping off, probably for the first time since it was wiggled onto her finger sixty-nine years ago. We are all just slipping through. We will all be released.

If you have grandparents, visit them. Go because no one will ever love you in the bold and gentle, big and uncomplicated way they do. Go because you can. Even if you think you can't, find a way. Take them up on their offer, let them wait for you at arrivals. Go because we all assume that what we have in our lives now, we will have in our lives forever. But the reality is we're only certain of our good fortune once we glimpse it in the rearview mirror. Go because you are loved. Go because you love. Go.

Let's Have the Wedding Later

I know, it's a big party. It is a pretty dress and a pretty cake and everyone is so very pretty because usually everyone is so very young. But what is the wedding all about, really? What have these two people even achieved? We met while we were hopeful and we were idiots, the best kind of idiots who have no idea of what's to come. We think we will handle everything thrown at us with aplomb and finesse. We are *different*, you see.

Unlike everyone who is giving us sage advice, we are actually more in love. Marriage will never be hard for us. We will always see our lover's side—because lovers is what we are right now, most of all—and we will respond to complaints with a level head and an open heart. We will never hold a grudge or raise a voice, and we will certainly never get divorced. Gross.

Look at us, crossing the finish line before the race has even started. We stand on the podium and beam as the gold medals are slung around our necks; we accept our bouquets and raise them above our heads long before the opening ceremony has taken place. No one trusts more in the crystal clear certainty of How Things Will Go more than us. We are winners. We have done it.

Except we have done nothing.

All we have done is agree we are in love and a party would be nice. We have achieved little except making our way through some checklists without murdering our parents or our florist. We have tasted the vegetarian options and we have chosen the wines. We have gathered wildflowers in mason jars and made elaborate chalk signs. We have posed this way and that. We have arrived. But, oh, we have so much to prove.

I know. Because we were once them. Weren't we all? But we are older now and know too much. Now we sit through wedding ceremonies (we are the "older family" or the "distant family" or the "workplace acquaintances") and at a particularly inane and unrealistic vow one of us will lean over and mutter to the other, "Good luck with that," and then we will try not to laugh, as if we are the children in that church.

So maybe the wedding should come later, when we can point around the room and at ourselves and to each other. "We made those two small people" we could say, and "You gave me these gray hairs" or "You nursed me back to health" and "You talked me down off the ledge more times than I can even count." *Thank you. I'm sorry. Let's party.*

We could write real vows based on real experience; they would sound like a cross between a eulogy, a performance review, and a thank-you card. We wouldn't worry about the future. We would talk about where we had been instead. We would propose carrying certain successful marriage initiatives forward. We would smile on both our past and present good fortune rather than moon over airy promises of future perfection.

I, take you, to continue being the person I am married to, more or less. We have changed and will continue to change but likely not in the same ways or at the same time and we've learned that's just how things go. We will cross those bridges as we get to them.

We do not "have" each other, since we are not objects to be possessed, and we don't always hold each other, because sometimes I just don't want to be touched, you know? But I get the general idea. And I assume you do too. Let's vow to continue on with that.

We can't know what will happen from this day forward, but I can say for sure we have experienced years of better and worse. So check and check on that front. And then we've experienced better again, because otherwise how could we be standing here right now?

We have been richer; we have been poorer; we have taken some stellar vacations and also borrowed money from our own children's savings accounts to bridge temporary ruin. We are aware how much fortune can smile and frown upon two people in one life together; we have experienced it in all its pants-shitting downturns and "A round for everyone in this bar!" glory.

We have personally been lucky, so far, to have experienced the survivable side of in sickness and in health. I'd like the record to show I prefer "in health." We have fielded calls from people we love as they share a grim diagnosis over the phone, like a telegram from hell. We have awaited test results, celebrated recovery, been to urgent care, been an outpatient, been scared, attended funerals. We have helped people we love as they lie dying, and nothing really prepares you for that; it's not what you think you're signing up for with this whole getting-married business. You think you're trying to select a shoe that gives you just the right height while also being something comfortable enough to dance in.

I promise to love and cherish you, although it can be hard to be pure about this, to be honest. Because I am always busy thinking about who needs new sneakers or snow pants and what are we going to do about camps next summer? I am thinking about whether our meals are well-balanced and if our kids will ever grow up to cross busy streets on their own because honestly I'm starting to have my doubts. I am thinking about the weight of having to steer this ship every day, mail the packages, greet the children in the morning versus yell at them, never miss a day of laundry or, oh Lord, will I regret it. Some days, most days, cherishing is pretty *far down the motherfucking list if you know what I'm saying. But I vow to bump it up a bit. At least above running a load of delicates.*

I promise to be better at just letting you help in the ways you help. Because ladies love to have help but then we want help in exactly the ways we would do things. So make the food this way and fold the towels that way, talk to the children like this and sunscreen them like that. And it all just begs the question, DO WE WANT HELP OR NOT?

But hey, speaking of vows, how about we vow to stop calling it "helping"? When I—a woman, the wife, the mother—am doing things, it is never referred to as "helping." I am not helping out around the house, I am not helping make ends meet, I am not helping raise our children. I am cleaning, mothering, working, doing. Such a variety of action verbs there! So no longer will I ask for help. I will expect you to just do—cut the grass, clean the kitchen, raise our children without babysitting them or watching them "for me."

Let's just do things, in our own particular ways, just so they get done already.

I don't know if death will ultimately be what parts us, but I hope for both our sakes that day is far away. Parting and death both. I say we do the best in the time we have, knowing what we know.

I would like to thank you, for loving me for so many years, which is insane when you think about it. You have loved me even when I have made extremely poor choices or given you highly sarcastic answers or no answers at all. You have loved me when I stormed out of our house/apartment/vacation rental. You have forgiven me for crying over manipulative commercials, and you have even forgiven me for criticizing you openly at parties.

You are still married to me even though, more than once, I have given you double middle fingers in the middle of a fight and told you to go fuck yourself—something I am certain I vowed I would never do when we were engaged.

Thank you for having sex with me so we could produce what are clearly a couple of the most stellar children we could've ever hoped for. These are our vows after all, and we should at least be allowed to brag a little.

Even given those excellent children and the highs and the lows, the tasks and the really good times, I would like to apologize for my heart calcifying over time. Maybe that's just the way things go. It is so hard to remain open and hopeful when you are a lady and getting older by the minute and also not a millionaire. What's there to be so damn cheerful about?

But I vow to try. That's the only vow I can really make at this point. Because having and holding and loving and cherishing feel like words from a fairy tale. And parting at death feels both dramatic and honestly pretty depressing. So I will vow to try. I will try not to blow my stack or throw my car keys across the room like I did that one time. Okay fine, those few times. I will try to look around more and appreciate what we have built together, this relationship, this life, and those children, because I'm going to mention them one more time; I can't help myself.

I promise I will be me from this day forward, and you will be you all the days of your life. I promise we will definitely get mad at each other and go to bed angry, we will also leave notes and text things like, "Everything will be okay" or "Hooray!" and "You're gonna do great, I know you will." I promise to keep trying, for as long as we both shall live.

I love you. Thank you. I'm sorry.

Let's party.

It's Complicated

"But you don't ever like anything I post on Facebook! You don't even look at my page!"

Those are not the words of a teenager, spitting ridiculous complaints across the room at her best friend or boyfriend. Those are the words of a forty-five-year-old woman, a mother of two, in the middle of a fight with her husband. A fight where the topic was divorce. Those were *my* words. As they shot out, I felt drenched in embarrassment, pathetic. To make sure the humiliation was complete, I started crying.

I couldn't have known twenty years ago on our wedding day, or when we got married again six months later at our "official" wedding with the white dress, dancing, and cans tied to the bumper of our getaway car, or during the many years afterward, but I was waiting for someone to invent social media.

Maybe when you grow up feeling unseen—by boys, by your parents, by the world—you will come away assuming any attention is good attention. And to get attention you need to put something out there. A variety of somethings. You must always be baiting the hook.

The introduction of e-mail had already allowed me to share and overshare. When my husband and I went on our monthlong road-trip honeymoon, I sent long group e-mails with recaps from the road to a couple dozen people, whether they wanted these e-mails or not. If that had been now, we'd have a sickeningly clever hashtag. And I'd blog and Instagram the absolute bejesus out of it all—the giant roadside tiger muskie in Minnesota, the peak foliage in Vermont, and the hurricanes we drank in New Orleans. Blessed.

I e-mailed reviews of disposable cameras I had tried out on another trip. I shared thoughts and stories and jokes. I made copies of photos for just about every single person who appeared in them and mailed them off with a card. It took real effort to keep people as one-way informed as I did.

When the moment I had been unknowingly waiting for finally arrived, it was my sister-in-law, of all people, who sent me the invite to join Facebook.

Duck, meet water.

For all my eventual mastery of the rat-a-tat-tat of social media, the mulling over of captions, and the needy exhibitionism, I had become consumed by what it told me I was missing. Better houses, better vacations, better bodies, better light, better weekends, but mostly, better marriages. My daily racetrack laps through the ether left me spinning. Had I had the best, most fun, most visually appealing day? Was I the funniest, the sharpest, the most liked? But more than anything, was I loved? I mean, loved enough for a bunch of random acquaintances to see?

That night, I splashed cold water on my hot face, pressing its coolness into my eyes, willing it to erase my insanity. I thought, *In a few years, I'll be teaching my kids how to navigate social media*—me.

Although I was the one who had brought up divorce, I wasn't suggesting we get divorced because of Facebook. I wasn't quite that unhinged. But I was holding Facebook up as evidence of how other husbands loved their wives in a way he didn't love me. I was suggesting we no longer loved each other, that this went both ways. I was suggesting I had become a different person; I had moved on, and it was clear he wasn't coming with me. I suggested every single part of this was obvious to everyone but him.

Jon is a carpenter, a builder, and a fixer of things. A listener of vinyl records and someone who does not like you opening a carton of milk if one is already open (I have the Post-it notes to prove it). He likes order but doesn't necessarily want to be in charge. He doesn't need to set the world on fire to get attention. And he married someone who was born with a can of gasoline in one hand and a book of matches in the other.

We were married in his parents' house, the house he grew up in, six months before his mother would succumb to the ovarian cancer that was slowly and painfully overtaking her body. At one point she turned to my father and said, "He will never hurt your daughter."

But it turns out not hurting each other in a marriage is impossible. Hurt comes from many places—the pervasive and low-hum hurt of unintentional neglect, the surprisingly damaging hurt of sarcasm taken too far, the near-catastrophic hurt of outside temptation, and the small nibbling hurt of not really seeing each other anymore. The days come and go; we are ghosts shuffling children through their checkpoints.

But when my father relayed her comment to me, I knew what she had meant. There is no one who doesn't love Jon. He is easygoing, quick to smile and slap you on the back in conversation (if you're a man) or gently squeeze your arm or hug you hard (if you're a woman). He loves his friends openly and deeply, never hesitating to jump in and help. He commands control over keeping our Ziploc containers and lids matched, he plants and tends our vegetable garden with our kids, and he takes them on long bike rides on hot summer Sundays. He looks like a younger Russell Crowe with a nicer smile and a happier childhood. He's a perfectionist at his job, capable and strong, a serious cook, and a believer in equally carrying the weight of raising our kids and taking care of our home.

When I hinted to my friends that we were in trouble, serious trouble, the struggling-for-empathy reactions all but said, "So you're an idiot, then?"

But that's the thing about love and marriage over time. There isn't much that's rational about it. The heart wants what it wants or doesn't want, and sometimes it wants the kind of attention that, in the big scheme of things, matters not at all. Sometimes it wants sparkly cartoon Band-Aids instead of the grim open-heart surgery it so desperately requires.

Up to that point, Facebook had served an actual purpose in my life. Living in Vermont and far from my coworkers and friends from previous jobs and cities, I used it to stay connected. As I scrambled to get freelance work going in the wake of being laid off, all of those old contacts and friends of friends flooded me with messages, supportive comments, project offers. The format and feedback loop of it fed my personal writing in a way nothing else had. And as I began working steadily from home, alone, I found social media was my way of having all the watercooler conversations without needing the watercooler. It was the perfect solution to everything I needed—conversation, networking, writing practice, connection, and inside jokes. And I didn't even need to shower.

I rationalized it was no different than spending half a day in meetings or on conference calls as I used to, it was just a different way of wasting time. But as the years went on, I shared more. All the time. Look at me! This is where I am! This is where I'm going! Hey, this is my opinion about this thing! And here's what I'm doing, *right now*! Pay attention to me, pay attention to me, but enough about me, why aren't *you* paying attention to me? At the same time, I willingly slid down a rabbit hole of competitive posting and hate reading, knowing better than most that social media doesn't equal real life but choosing to accept it all at face value anyway.

The world I was connected to became simultaneously bigger (my network grew) and smaller (I barely interacted with most of my neighbors or parents at my kids' school). In the process, my sense of what a normal marriage was—if there even is such a thing—became pretty distorted.

On Facebook everyone had their own television show, dramedies shot through with spot-on humor and the tidiest locations, all set during the warm forgiving light of magic hour. Don't even try being as in love as someone who posts about it constantly on Facebook. Because no one has ever been or will ever be that in love. Not you. And certainly not me. And in my own way I was just as guilty. I was my own showrunner, but for a show my husband had no interest being cast in. It was a show I starred in with guest appearances by my kids and our hapless cat, Oreo. It wasn't ideal, but as with all midseason replacements, we tried to make it work.

The night we talked more about the possibilities of divorce, Jon responded to my loop the loop of questioning in the only way he knew how—like a noncrazy rational person. He never posted anything on Facebook; he didn't really look at anyone's page; he doesn't comment or like anything; he barely even checks it! But that wasn't the point. That wasn't what this was all about.

What I was too ashamed to say in those moments was, "Why don't you understand me?" and "Why can't you love me more?" and most selfishly, "And why can't you let everyone know it while you're at it?"

Why can't you crave attention too?

But that wasn't the person I had married. He had never been that person. He hadn't changed since I met him. I had changed, and the world had changed around him. He doesn't gush or send me GIFs. The first time I texted him a thumbs-up emoji he replied,

"That's not very nice," because he thought I was saying "Up yours."

What I had forgotten were all the times he had come home from work with flowers to celebrate good news or ice cream to help soothe the bad. Or the many times I told him I was going to be away for two weeks for work or head to Maine for a weekend to write or even quit my job and he said, "Go for it." Sure, those are sporadic examples, spread out over years. But from the minute we started dating, I have earned more than him, my job has taken priority over his, and anything I've set out to do he has supported without question. It's astounding, really. He has never guilted me into being anyone other than who I am, and if you knew me you might question him on that particular point. He has never asked me to tone down this whole breadwinner business. He has never needed me to bolster his masculine image, because he has had the inner confidence and stability he was raised with all along. He has never needed a virtual pat on the back for any reason. Frankly, it was a wonder we had made it this far.

He is an excellent father, a great friend, a good man.

He doesn't care if he looks cool—as a photo taken on the beach this past summer proves, with his sunglasses placed over his supermarket readers and one of our kids' bucket hats perched too small upon his head—and it'll be a cold day in hell before he takes a selfie or arranges things on the floor for a photo. He's not an Instagram husband. But he is my husband. And marriages aren't made to be contained in 140 characters or look better with just the right filter. Because it was already pretty good, I just wasn't looking up enough to see what was right in front of me.

We didn't magically solve anything that night three years ago when we talked about divorce. We didn't instantly fall back in love. I didn't quit Facebook. But by allowing myself to feel imperfect and stupid in a way I had outlawed on social media, I had shocked myself into seeing how unrealistic—and dangerous—my expectations had become. A few of the couples whose theoretical happiness I had wallowed in split up. We all see what we want to see, even when there's nothing there. Or maybe especially when there's a lot there that can't be neatly contained in a single photo, even with the longest of captions.

Our marriage has absolutely changed over time, because people change over time. None of us expect to be cradled in the nook of someone's arm like an infant until we die. We don't crawl or stumble around like stiff-legged drunks to go to our jobs. We walk, we run, we take the hits as we keep going, paying the toll for every year we pass. We are encouraged to climb, climb higher, be better, do great things. What are the odds that two people do that in the exact same way, on the same trajectory, with the same level of ambition or desire or capacity for change? What are the odds it all works out just fine?

When we stood in that tiny church in front of our family and friends I can guarantee I wasn't thinking about how I would handle motherhood or what turning forty might do to me. I wasn't thinking about how maybe that thing about our sex lives taking a nosedive might not be a cliché or that fights over the most absurdly minor things could go nuclear and sweep up our very existence in their paths.

I was mostly thinking about cutting that cake and how I looked in my dress and how we had done it. We had really done it. I had done it. I was married! And if anyone had given us any sage advice (which they did, they wrote it down at our reception, I still have all of it) I wouldn't have listened.

"It's complicated." That's what Facebook gave us, to some more than others.

We took a break from talking about divorce. That's not to say we have Saturday-morning prebreakfast sex or hazy late nights in strip-club parking lots in my '65 Chevy like we did when we were first married. But we're planning a twentieth-anniversary party I wasn't convinced we'd ever see. I no longer look to Facebook as an authority on much, especially love. And I have stopped looking at other marriages entirely, because the combination of two people who aren't us is irrelevant. It's like listening to birth stories at your baby shower. It has nothing to do with you; it never did.

So much is gone now. That Chevy. His parents. Too many friends to count. Our twenties, and our thirties. But we're still here. We are still here. And as I stand in this spot, much as I did on that day in that tiny church, I can't at all predict what turning fifty will do to me, or what will happen when our children leave home. I don't know whether we will survive it as a team vowing to take on the storm together or if we will inevitably drift and break apart. I don't know, because my incessant requests for a crystal ball keep going unanswered.

But I do know it took two decades of marriage and eight years of social media to realize I'm someone who has always needed a stage to stand on. And it took almost blowing everything up to remember I married someone who has always been happy to build that stage for me, carefully and quietly. Just the way he wants to, in the background.

So what we do now is hold on. Hold on to what has gotten us this far, hold on to whatever has made us a successful combination of sameness and difference, and hold on to those things that pass between us with just a knowing look. We can try to do what our parents hoped we would—not hurt each other.

What I can do is not look to other people we barely know for answers, and instead, finally, read all that advice that was written down in a wave of wine-soaked happiness so long ago. The advice that didn't have character limits or filters, the advice that was private and from people who loved us.

I could log in to real life.

TIME-OUT

Your Cute Wedding Hashtags
Twenty Years Later

#DoYouHaveAnyCashOnYou
#DidYouWriteACheckOutOfTheJointAccount
#CanYouPickUpMilkAndWineOnTheWayHome
#AndIceCream
#ShitAreYouStillAtTheMarket
#AndThatRiceMixYouKnowTheOneILikeItsInABlackBag
#OhAndLaundryDetergent
#UghAndToiletPaperNevermindIllJustGoLater
#AreYouGoingToShave
#AreYouGoingToWearThatShirt
#NoReason
#WhatAboutThosePants
#WhatsTheStoryWithThoseShoes
#ThatDressLooksFineLetsGo
#WhatsWithTheToothpasteEverywhere
#AndTheToiletSeatSituation
#WhatIsHappening
#WouldItKillYouToMakeTheBed
#What
#Nothing
#IDidntSayAnything
#ThereWasntAToneInMyVoice
#NoThereWasnt

#TheDishwasherIsBroken
#TheFurnaceIsntWorking
#TheToiletIsClogged
#TheBasementIsFlooding
#HaveYouLeftWorkYet
#RememberItsGirlsNightOut
#YesIDidTellYou
#IToldYouTwoWeeksAgo
#YouDontListen
#Whatever
#WhateverWhatever
#DidYouCallTheDoctor
#DidYouBringTheCarIn
#DidYouCallThePlaceAboutTheThing
#UghCanIHaveSomeBlankets
#YesItISColdInHere
#StopTellingMeHowIFeel
#YesYouDo
#YouDo
#OHMYGOD
#BrinkOfDivorce
#WeSeeATherapistNow
#WeValidateEachOthersFeelings
#AllTheTime
#ItsExhausting
#CouldItBeUntilCrabbinessDoWePartInstead
#WhatHaveWeDone
#HappyAnniversaryToUs
#Suckers
#SeriouslyDontForgetTheWineAtTheMarket

Kids, It's Time You Knew the Truth— Your Mother Is a Real Piece of Work

Look, I know you guys have sensed something's wrong, even though we've tried hard to hide all of . . . *this* . . . from you. We just didn't want you to worry. But we can't really get anything past you two, can we? You guys are just too smart.

Your mother has been to a lot of specialists, and trust me when I say we've been working really hard trying to find answers. And, yes, I know we've shooed you away from our private conversations, but that ends today. You deserve to know the truth. There's no easy way to say this other than to just, you know, come right out and say it. So, here it is:

Your mother is a Real Piece of Work.

. . .

Sorry, just needed to take a deep breath there, a really deep breath. Wow, it's finally out there. I can't believe it.

I'm sure you have a lot of questions, I know I did. First, let me say there's still a lot we don't know right now. We're not sure how her condition might progress over time or if there was something we could've done to prevent it. Honestly, we may never know.

For example, when we were planning our wedding I let her not only choose what the groomsmen would wear but also what my new last name would be and where we would live. Looking back, I can't help but wonder if maybe I shouldn't have let her do any of that. As if I had that kind of control back then. Or even now. Don't make me laugh!

Or when you were born, Julie. She said, "I love the name Julie!" and I said, "Well, I'm not really a fan of that name, how about Charlotte or Amanda?" And she responded, "So it's settled, Julie it is."

What? No. No! I'm not saying I don't like your name! I mean, that's what I was saying back *then*. Of course I love your name; I love *you*, that's what really matters doesn't it? I do like your name. Yes, I do. Forget what I just said. Honey, don't look at me like that. NO, I'M NOT CALLING YOU HONEY BECAUSE I HATE THE NAME JULIE.

Sorry, lost my cool there for a minute. It's just this . . . *situation* . . . has really taken a toll on me. For years I was beating myself up thinking her condition was due to something I had done or not done, that maybe I didn't love her enough or in the way she needed to be loved, that this was somehow all my fault. It's such a relief to finally have some answers.

Don't roll your eyes at me.

That reminds me, we don't know if your mother's condition is hereditary. I'm no medical doctor or, as it turns out, even a halfway decent insurance adjuster, but if I had to guess I'd say it skips a generation. Your grandmother? Lovely woman! Lovely. Your great-grandmother? Hoo boy, you needed to put a sweater on when she came into a room because it got *cold* in there, if you catch my drift.

No, not catching it? I'm saying she was a total bitch, you guys. That's what I'm saying. I'm sorry, I'm sorry. That was obviously inappropriate. I mean, I stand by my assessment of her condition, if not my particular phrasing of it. Obviously things back then weren't nearly as sophisticated as they are today, from a diagnostic perspective. But my layperson's hunch is that your great-grandmother was also a Real Piece of Work.

That aside, I'm sure you're wondering what our next steps are and what can be done. As far as I've been able to figure out, there's no actual cure for your mother's condition. She will continue to be a Real Piece of Work for the rest of her life. She was a Real Piece of Work when we met, and, if anything, this is one area of her life where she's been remarkably consistent. And completely oppressive.

I've had a lot of time to reflect on this and I do think there could be a silver lining to this whole situation. We'll finally have a name to put with her condition. Instead of just thinking—and I'll speak for myself here—that we'll never be good enough for her or that we're horrible people, we can all just know, deep down, it's simply because she's a Real Piece of Work.

It reminds me of my boss, who has a condition called Born Rich and Doesn't Really Need This Job. Every time I think, *Man, why am I always the one who's working late, grabbing him a coffee, making excuses for why he can't be at a meeting?* That's when I remind myself he can't help it—it's just that he was Born Rich and Doesn't Really Need This Job. It helps, it honestly does.

I guess what I'd like to emphasize as we sort this all out is that we need to take care of ourselves. Just do whatever you need to do to feel happy and sane. You might not believe this, but I've gotten back into painting and I've been doing a lot of reading as well.

Recently I came across this poem and I'd like to read it to you girls. I think it might help us reframe our predicament. But I guess, to be accurate, I didn't just "come across" it; I actually rewrote it. Okay, fine, I stole it. The original is called "Welcome to Holland." Maybe you've heard of it?

My version is called "Welcome to Hell." I hope you like it.

Welcome to Hell

I am often asked to describe the experience of living with someone who's a Real Piece of Work—to try to help people who have not shared this unique experience to understand it, to imagine how it would feel. It's like this . . .

When you're getting married, it's like planning a fabulous party—in a bar, on a floating barge, to Sex Land. You buy a bunch of "guidebooks" and make your wonderful plans. The Reverse Cowgirl, the Naughty Financial Adviser, the Rent Is Two Months Late, and Someone Needs a Spanking. It's all very exciting.

After months of eager anticipation, the day finally arrives. You pack your bags and off you go. Several hours later, the plane lands. The stewardess comes in, tongue flickering, hands raised in devil horns, and she whisper-shouts, "Welcome to hell."

"Hell?!" you say. "What do you mean, hell? I signed up for Sex Land! I'm supposed to be in Sex Land. All my life I've dreamed of going to Sex Land!"

But there's been a change in the flight plan. They've landed in hell and there you must stay.

The important thing is they haven't taken you to some horrible, disgusting, filthy place, full of pestilence,

famine, and disease. OR HAVE THEY? IT'S CALLED
HELL AFTER ALL.

*So, shit, now you have to go out and buy a new
guidebook. And you have to learn a whole bunch of new
facial expressions. And you will meet a whole new group
of people you would never have met—or you* would *have
if your wife hadn't alienated every last one of them.*

*It's just a different place. It's much more hell-y than
Sex Land, way less fun than Sex Land. But after you've
been there for a while and you catch your breath, you
look around, and you begin to notice hell has a lot of
sighing, hell has inexplicable rage, hell even has the most
biting judgments; it just honestly takes your breath away
sometimes. This place sucks.*

*Meanwhile, everyone you know is busy coming and
going from Sex Land, and they're all bragging about
what a wonderful time they had there.* God, *you think,*
my friends are total dicks. *And for the rest of your life
you will say, "Ugh, that's where I was supposed to go.
That's what I had planned."*

*The pain of that will never, ever, go away, because the
loss of that dream will make you want to stab your so-
called friends. Right in their parts.*

*But if you spend your life mourning the fact that you
didn't get to Sex Land, you may never be free to enjoy the
very special hell that is hell.*

You know what, now that I read this out loud, this poem is stupid. It's not helping at all.

Fuck Holland.

Fuck hell.

Fuck your mother.

Someone should.

SHOWDOWNS

Overshare

My phone currently contains more than thirty-eight thousand photos and seven hundred videos.

This digital shit storm doesn't take into account the pre-iPhone film photos or even the digital-camera ones, nor does it include the videos on my desktop, laptop, and floating across multiple clouds (What *are* clouds? Does anyone even know?). It doesn't include what's on Instagram or across all the photo-editing apps I've since abandoned. And of course it can't include the hundreds of shots I wished I had taken and did not.

It's like Wayne Gretzky said, "You miss one hundred percent of the shots you don't take."

When my kids were little, I worried I was documenting them too much, which didn't stop me from actually doing it. Not even a little bit. I was training them to the camera, like circus lions to the whip. I needed every smile, every outfit, every crazy-hair morning, every beach, every Popsicle, every ice cream cone, every new book, every hat, every snowman, every Christmas Eve, every birthday, every sparkly dress, every Lego, every first day of school, every last day of school, every morning, every afternoon, every moment of every day of their lives. Line up against this wall, this mural, this place where the light is better.

I worried about the end game here. What *was* the end game here? I kept telling myself everyone else was doing it too, so it must be okay. I was using an adolescent argument for a very grown-up problem.

Now that my kids are older, and as I continue to try to tease this apart, I can see I was conflating documenting with sharing. Because I wasn't just documenting moments so I could savor them down the road or press them in a book, I was documenting moments in order to share them, and share them *immediately*. It wasn't enough for us to know we went blueberry picking, everyone else must also know we went blueberry picking. And not just blueberry picking but blueberry picking on a beautiful day in Vermont, rolling hills and puffy white clouds very much in evidence. Behold my children wearing good outfits and showing their adorable faces and those curls or eyes or chubby fingers. Look at us! We are *killing it* over here! Aren't we? Please like this photo.

I have occasionally followed basic ethical guidelines for photography, like asking my kids for their permission to take a photo. The problem with that is they will sometimes say no and isn't that a pickle? So I have also taken many, many more photos of them without asking. I have begged them. I have paid them a dollar and once paid them each three dollars. I have asked them nicely and I have guilted them into it.

The documenting that would often cause the most friction were the shots I wanted to take as we raced out the door to something, when they looked their cutest, their most dressed up, or were fully engulfed in costumes. When we were on our way to An Event. We would always end up running late, as my kids posed and jumped and finally ran out of the frame and away from me.

The best moments were when we worked together, picking outfits or settings for a photo, or creating different roles and scenarios for videos. There was one period in particular when I struggled to hold myself together as a dear friendship imploded. I never wanted to return home after school because that's when the loneliness would hit me, as we all went our separate ways. I needed them with me; I needed them close, to try to dull how alone I felt. For weeks on end, I'd pick them up from school and we'd take off on afternoon adventures. We'd pick raspberries or walk through the woods. We'd wander in sunflower fields and drive to small-town libraries forty-five minutes away. I wanted to be away from everyone I knew, everyone except them. I was attempting to escape the ache in my life, and although they didn't know it, my kids were consoling me with their presence. Simply by being in this with me.

One memorable afternoon, I brought along the giant costume tree heads Jon and I had bought at a library tag sale when we first moved to Vermont. The kids and I traipsed through the woods and stood in front of barns, pretending to be autumn trees. It was completely silly. And really wonderful. Sharing took on this veneer of "Here I am, and I am fine. I am doing fine. See me? I'm doing great." It was a way of signaling to people who didn't even care anymore that I would survive this. A breakup is a breakup is a breakup.

Although it's difficult all these years later to look at those photos without feeling incredibly sad, I also cherish them because they represent my kids and I creating something together. It felt healing. There was no work, no homework, no chores, no unfriending, no sadness, and no life outside the three of us. At least for a couple of hours each day.

But the worst moments were profoundly, almost unspeakably, awful. Those were the times when I crossed the line, when I got so frustrated that I utterly blew my stack. Over a photo. For Facebook. There is one photo in particular that always springs to mind. It's of my daughter when she was about five years old.

We had picked up a mini watermelon from the farmers' market after school and I wanted to get a photo of her holding it when we got home. She complained it was too heavy, she didn't want to hold it, she wanted to go inside, and when she shifted it ever so slightly it almost slipped from her hands. I screeched, "DON'T YOU DARE DROP THAT WATERMELON."

Oh my God.

She burst into tears. I still have the photo from right before that moment. The worst I ever feel as a parent is when I come across it during an archival dig. It tells me everything I've ever done wrong with her in exactly one frame. A little kid. A powerful adult. Me bending her to my will. Her not strong enough to even hold this tiny smooth watermelon. Me yelling at her for almost dropping it. *All for a photo.*

I know I shared that photo. I know it got some likes—how many, who knows now. I know my daughter still remembers that moment, even all these years later. How could she not? Even still, I'm afraid to ask her, to conjure that ghost. And I know it was never even remotely worth it. What was happening to me there? What was I hoping for?

There is a hunger to share our children with the world or even just our supposedly private circle (nothing is private, *nothing*). They are special to us, and we want everyone else to think they're special too. Can't you see it? Just look at them! Swimming and jumping across hay bales, graduating from preschool and eating birthday cake. Can't you see it too? Would you please like this photo to prove to me you also see how wonderful they are? Would you please encourage me to do more of this sort of thing? Let's admire my children together.

Another time, another utter failure of my position. My kids, just two and four, had tagged along with me when I voted for Barack Obama in 2008. Now *that* was a day. When we arrived at our polling place, I took a photo of them standing next to the VOTE—ENTER HERE sign as they shouted "Vote! Vote! Vote!" to passersby. My son wore a cowboy hat and his red puffy vest. And she wore a handmade paper crown, pink pants, and held her orange-and-white stuffed kitty named Milky. She was rocking on the sides of her feet, her little white Converse on rubber edge in the photo.

Four years later. As we prepared to repeat that voting field trip, I mentioned how we should try to re-create the original photo as accurately as we could. That it would be fun to see how much they'd grown, that it was important to mark this incredible occasion, for them, for us as a family, but let's face it, mostly for me. I printed out the old photo. We found my son's old cowboy hat. My daughter plucked Milky from her bed, the one thing that hadn't yet been outgrown.

They were more self-conscious this time, especially as my eight-year-old son popped a cowboy hat on his head that he had last worn when he was four, half a lifetime ago. And my daughter held her stuffed kitty Milky, although her ivory cable sweater dress and knee-high leather boots gave her the look of a teenager instead of the child she still was. I tried to take the photo fast, to not get in the way of other people attempting to dash in and out to cast their vote. I tried to get my kids to look in the same direction as they did in that old photo or to hold hands the same way, not too tight, just a little bit loose. Neither of them really wanted to do it. They were distracted by all the activity, embarrassed by the attention, just wanting to be done with it already. Still, they soldiered on, albeit a bit more vocally. My daughter, especially, put up a stink about it. She is always the one unafraid to put up a stink about things.

I had promised we would get cupcakes after this whole thing, if they would just cooperate. I knew we were in bribery territory, and I was more than okay with it. It wasn't the first time and it certainly wouldn't be the last.

But my daughter kept messing around. She was tired and whiny. She didn't want to cooperate. Or at least that's what I thought was happening as she seemed to be squirming around with her legs and her feet and not standing up tall. Christ. I finally snapped, "STOP DOING THAT. YOU'RE NOT GETTING A CUPCAKE AFTER THIS."

Oh my God.

OH MY GOD.

Of course she cried. Of course she did! What a goddamn monster! And through her tears she said, *"I was . . . trying . . . to have my foot . . . the way it was . . . in the old picture."*

Are you trying to figure out which part is worse? Because it's five years later and I'm still not sure. Was it me yelling? Or me threatening to take away her cupcake? Maybe it was the fact that even though she didn't want to, she was posing for that photo anyway? And not only posing, but trying to make her six-year-old foot rock to the side in the same exact position as her two-year-old foot? Or was it that she had studied the photo and was doing her hardest to replicate it? And I yelled at her. And she was six. And I'm a grown-up and I yelled at her.

I am such a fucking asshole.

I'm looking at that photo now. And my heart feels utterly broken. It feels broken for how far down a rabbit hole I had to be to think that was normal-person behavior. It feels broken for how far down a rabbit hole I still am. It feels broken for how much I trained my children to stop what they were doing, to hold up the flower, the mud pie, the shell, the feather. To stand in the sunset, no this way, no that way, jump! Run! Now do it again!

Would I have taken so many photos if I hadn't planned on sharing them? I can guarantee I wouldn't have. That's not to say I wouldn't have taken any. I originally became interested in photography when my dad gave me my first camera in junior high. I graduated from college with a bachelor of fine arts in photography. This isn't a new interest or hobby; it didn't float up from the Internet and snatch me in its evil grasp. I have always been looking for patterns and possibilities. But there are no longer any consequences for taking a million photos. We have completely lost the time and cost barriers of dropping off film, paying for prints, and tracking our negatives. You never knew what shots you had. And unless you were a professional photographer with an unlimited film budget, you wouldn't keep firing away on a motor drive until you got what you came for.

But when you combine the ease of taking endlessly free digital photos with something that is always on you, the ability to share those images instantly from that same thing in your pocket, and then let's go ahead and frost that whole shit cake with a feedback loop that only encourages you to do it more? Well.

When we document simply for the pleasure of doing so, for our own use and satisfaction, I believe we are more likely to let moments unfold. To capture what is happening in front of us versus engineering what we want to happen. It's the difference between a documentary and a reality show. Not always, not every time. There have been posed group shots, first-day-of-school snaps, and "Hold up your Christmas present!" photos since photography became accessible to the masses. But the addition of interaction and validation has blurred the lines completely and permanently.

There is pleasure in letting yourself be known. There is satisfaction that even given all the (highly stylized, highly fictionalized) evidence of your life, others approve. And especially as mothers, as women, I believe there is a desire to be seen. We go from being so visible during our pregnancies to being shoved aside the minute our babies are born. We step back into the shadows as the light—and attention, resources, and time—shine down upon our children. Perhaps it is a way of reclaiming our space or some semblance of self. And maybe that's all just bullshit and we're simply hungry for validation. Like I'm the expert.

I'm also not a psychic, I have no ability to see ten or twenty or thirty years into the future. I can't anticipate what all of this documenting and sharing has done to my kids. I only know what it's done to me. The sheer volume of photos I take of them has dropped steeply with each passing year, although no one on social media would likely be able to tell the difference. They are getting older, more aware of their digital presence. And I have stopped competing with other parents online, to try to get the better photo of that thing our kids all do. Whatever it is.

I have tried harder to be respectful of what they want and what they don't want. I'm often taken aback when they ask me to take a photo or video of something they're doing. And I can't help but feel the deepest sense of irony when I actually hear myself say, "You know you don't need to take a photo of everything you do."

These are more or less the same words they have said to me dozens of times in the past. When they were younger. When I wouldn't listen.

Now that they are dipping their toes into social media and looking for their own content to share, it's jarring how often I'm even tangentially included in a photo or a video that I didn't know they were taking and I screech, "Delete that now! Don't you dare post that!" I can't help but feel sheepish, knowing the tables are very much turned, that they deserved that same autonomy and power over their image and their lives.

When you get right down to it, I felt that their likenesses, their words, their quips, and sadness all belonged to me. Maybe

I felt that way because at one point, they *were* me. And then, once they were born, I poured everything I had into them. The hours of mothering are long and tedious. So when those moments of joy, beauty, laughter, and utter nonsense would bubble up, I wanted to hold them up. I thought those moments were all mine to share.

Randomly throughout the years, they have been approached at barbecues and on beaches, at houses of friends even hours away from where we live, by people they've never met, and those strangers have repeated back to them moments in their lives. Riding a horse for the first time, going on vacation, finishing school. How fucked up is that? Moments in their lives when just the two or three or four of us were present, were opened up to five hundred other people. Without their consent.

And yet here's the thing: when I page back through these tens of thousands of photos and hundreds of videos, I see not just their lives but *our* lives, together. The stuffies and favorite shoes I had forgotten about, and just how little they used to be. There are the snowflakes-on-eyelashes in December and the mud-pie making in August. These are the small moments, the unposed moments. The long drives and the missing teeth. These are moments that would've been lost to me, guaranteed. I like having evidence of these moments.

One time I was paging through the previous year's worth of photos as I hastily assembled a calendar for a Christmas gift. As I edited my way through the months, past the sledding in February and Easter-egg hunts in April, Maine in the summertime and apple pies in September, I whispered to myself, "We have a good life. We have had a good life."

My childhood was anonymous. Almost all of ours were. And I have raised my kids publicly. Not transparently, but publicly. I'm not sure what I will tell them if they ask me why I did that, why all of us did that, what was the point? It's difficult to navigate something you have only experienced as an adult, something you did not grow up with and therefore don't have the same developmental experience of.

I suppose I will be honest with them. I will tell them that documenting them in all these ways made me proud, made me laugh, allowed me to connect with other parents and family and friends who were far away. It also drove me to make terrible and selfish decisions, because I lost sight of who they were and the rights they had. Because I was so deep in a second adolescence, where I was desperately seeking validation and approval. Where I did what everyone else did, more than everyone else did, so that it would all reflect back on me without consideration for how they might feel.

I will tell them there is no easy answer. That on one hand I'm sorry, I made some appalling mistakes, I will do better. And that on the other, I'm happy I have all those pictures of them. I can't regret that. I will tell them that sharing is what we all learned to do in kindergarten, but this newish form of sharing is the furthest thing from that spirit. When we are young we are taught to share to form community, to even out resources, and to feel good through giving. Now we are enticed to share to build ourselves up at the expense of others, like by like, into a castle with no foundation. A castle built on clouds.

Thank You for Including Me on This Meal Train but Unfortunately I'm a Horrible Person

Hello, practically a stranger!

Although I've only seen your name under the People You May Know tab on Facebook, it seems you've roped me into a social obligation from which there is no graceful escape. I'm sure you assumed—since I'm a good friend of our mutual friend—that I share her more wonderful qualities like kindness, culinary skills, and the ability to find joy in feeding others. Well, would you believe I don't possess any of those? You would if you actually knew me.

I want this to be a learning experience for both of us but mainly for you. So I'm responding with a multiple-choice quiz that you may take at your leisure. Should I invite some of your tangential acquaintances to take it too? Maybe while they're at it they could make you a meal and feel resentful about it? Anyway, I hope you'll find this quiz useful, at least more useful than I plan on being in this lifetime.

CAN YOU CORRECTLY GUESS MY REACTIONS TO BEING ADDED TO THIS FUCKING MEAL TRAIN?: A QUIZ

1. I couldn't help but notice you've included me on this Meal Train for a mutual friend of ours who just:

    a) Had a baby.
    b) Suffered a death in the family.
    c) Wait, what happened? Seems if I don't even know what happened, I'm probably not close enough friends with this person and therefore should definitely, definitely not be on this Meal Train. How did you find me?
    d) Bought a house. Did it not come with a kitchen? Seems like a buyer-beware situation to me.
    e) I literally don't care.

2. Of course my first reaction was:

    a) Uuuuuuuggggggghhhhhhhhh NO. No!
    b) Bitch, I can't even properly prepare meals for my own family as it is.
    c) Maybe I never saw this.
    d) I'm gonna act like I never saw this.
    e) I did not see this.

3. Then reality struck and I:

    a) Forced myself to add some cheerful comment as confirmation I have received this fucking thing. Ugh, fuck this fucking thing.
    b) Momentarily deluded myself for five whole minutes by believing I can actually do this—Look at me everyone, I'm turning over a new leaf! One where I make a complete and

delicious meal as a gesture of support and non-assholeness
on behalf of my friend in need! I am a good person!

c) I am not a good person.

d) Accepted that even my kids know I don't say, "I love you
and I'm here for you" with food. It's more like, "Maybe you
could stay alive for another day?"

e) Clapped twice and summoned the pizza menus.

4. And finally, I:

a) Will wait as long as possible to commit to a date, hoping
whatever the issue is has resolved itself by then.

b) Will text with other horrible people about our shared Meal
Train rage. Trust me, it's a thing.

c) Will sheepishly search for articles about Meal Train
etiquette because if I'm going to do this, I'm not gonna lose
face over it. Fuck that shit.

d) Will flip out when I realize the meal needs to be dairy-free.
What in the ever-loving Christ?

e) Will order pizza anyway in a shot-heard-round-the-world
act of sabotage that broadcasts, "I'm obviously not very
good at this, and I might possibly even accidentally kill
people, so maybe no one should include me on one of
these things ever, ever again."

5. And then I spent a few days attempting to think deeply on this
act of forcible community support and why it made me so nuts.
Turns out I could think shallowly about it and end up at the same
place, which was:

a) I see a lot of women's names on these things. And by "a
lot of women's names" I mean *only* women's names. Meal

Trains, bake sales, potlucks, all those kitchen-y bake-y cook-y things. Is this what the 1950s were like? Because if so, I'm here to tell you the 1950s sucked.

b) Do men not know how to plan and cook a meal? The fact that out of over one hundred Michelin three-star restaurants only six have female chefs certainly tells me otherwise. Or do men only know how to cook the fancy, prestigious meals that come with press coverage?

c) Do there really need to be etiquette articles about this whole mess? How not only is the straight-up donation of one's time, money, and effort not good enough but you should also really try to switch up the meal choices, do something not only unexpected but also excellent and something everyone from two years old to their great-grandparents will like. Guaranteed. Don't drop off dishes that need to be returned, bring enough food for everyone but not *too* much or there won't be any room left in the refrigerator, oh and maybe bring flowers or a gift for the oldest kid and definitely some ice cream and WHAT THE FUCK IS THIS SHIT? Do you want help or not? Maybe we could all chip in and buy you a restaurant and a farmers' market instead? Maybe for your birthday you could tell me everything you don't like in advance and then afterward tell me everything that was wrong with the gift I gave you?

d) Stop. Assuming. All women. Cook. Or have the time to cook. OH MY GOD.

e) I told you I was horrible.

ANSWER KEY: All. Especially e's. Unsubscribe.

Your Participation Trophies Are Bullshit

It was the end of horseback-riding camp and my daughter clip-clopped over to me in her dirt-and-manure-encrusted boots. She held up her two ribbons, one red and one blue. She singled out the blue one and said, "You don't like this one, do you?"

"Of course I don't. You got that one just for breathing."

She knows how I feel about awards or ribbons or trophies or certificates or shout-outs just for the sake of recognizing a child is among the living and has managed to drag his or her carcass to camp, to a game or practice, to the play, to class, through life. I don't know where this whole thing started, but I don't like it.

I thought this was something that sprung up in the 90s and we all made fun of now. I actually thought we were over it, especially in this age of resilience and grit and other Super-Important Parenting Buzzwords. But then my kids signed up for the elementary school play and I had to attend the mandatory parent meeting. If there's one thing I can't get enough of it's mandatory parent meetings. Especially the kind that happen at night, right around dinnertime. Oh baby.

I sat there leafing through multiple handouts, a complicated calendar, and rules containing several points of **<u>EMPHASIS IN UNDERLINE, BOLD, AND ALL CAPS</u>**. My kids were only in fourth and fifth grade, not on Broadway. Couldn't they just throw on an old cat costume and call it a day? Maybe one of them could be a sun, I don't know.

As the women leading the meeting made clear, every kid who wanted to be in the play would be in the play. Every kid would have a role. We're talking more than a hundred kids. Every kid in fourth and fifth grade would get speaking lines, guaranteed. They had counted all the lines in the script and divided them by grade and number of kids. The higher grades getting more lines and singing solos and the lower grades getting the smaller parts. But! No one should emphasize big versus little speaking roles. All roles were important. There are no big parts!

Um. But. There *are* big parts.

I took it all in, thinking back on my own experiences of participating in plays in school. I had to take both hands and push my jaw back up into place. I looked around the room so I could lock eyes with other like-minded parents. We'd definitely give each other that look that said, "WHAT THE HELL IS THIS?" There was no way I could be the only one bewildered by the fact there'd be three Simbas and three Nalas. Why was every supporting character in *The Lion King* exploded into a gang of multiples with rhyming names? What was even happening here?

I looked around the room, scanning faces for that look of recognition and I saw . . . nothing. Absolutely nothing. Not a face turned toward mine, not a single parent who looked surprised or upset by this information. In fact, several had their notebooks out or their phones open to a notes app as they jotted down the dictated information. Some asked follow-up questions like, "When you say 'small' role, how many lines would that be?" or "Number of lines–wise, what is the difference between a small and medium speaking part?"

WHAT ARE YOU EVEN SAYING? My Chipotle order is ready, let's wrap this fucking cuckoo fest up.

When I returned home, I dumped my color-coded printouts,

the calendar, the permissions slips, and all the rules out onto the kitchen counter.

"This is *absurd*. Do you realize you have a speaking part no matter what?"

"Yes!" my daughter answered brightly.

"No," I went on. "That's just so wrong. So wrong! That's not how plays work in the real world. That's not how anything works in the real world. You're supposed to try out for a play. The kids who are the best actors or actresses and singers get the best and biggest parts. Oh, I forgot, there are no big parts," I added sarcastically.

She just shrugged. For some reason kids don't love monologues.

I know this participation-trophy approach didn't start with this particular theater company, and it didn't start with the owners of the horse farm where my daughter attended camp. Schools and organizations—anyone dealing with kids—have been trained by almost three decades of parents to recognize children blindly and equally. No matter how much they suck.

We do our children a disservice when we support this narrative. When we tell them they're great at everything, excellent at whatever they attempt, good job! Kids are smart. They look to us for truth. When we tell them something that doesn't totally jibe with their perception and experience, what does that say about us? That, at the minimum, we're kind of liars?

I'm not suggesting we come at them boot camp-style and scream about everything they're terrible at. What I am suggesting is we take steps to free our teachers, schools, camp leaders, coaches, instructors, other parents, and culture (pretty easy, right?) from enforcing this fairy tale that every kid is exceptional and perfect. Because it is not true. You know it; I know it. Everyone knows it. Kids definitely know it. They can pick out which kid is the killer soccer player, an incredible artist, a big-time reader. Saying "So are you!" isn't just wrong, it belittles true achievement.

Sure, everyone should be able to take a crack at something they've never tried before. This is what ultimately made me back off my school-play flip-out. I had to recognize I was comparing elementary school with high school—clearly not a fair comparison. Every kid in elementary school should get a chance to be in a play. Does it have to be a play where a production truck is parked outside the gym during tech-rehearsal week? Debatable. I'm not sure I even heard the phrase *tech rehearsal* before my junior year of high school. But every kid certainly deserves a shot to create, to compete, and to push themselves in whatever way they choose.

They should also be able to trust that when they win something, they have won it fair and square—through studying hard, loads of discipline, or lots of practice. They should be able to own it deep in their bones. They should know it's real.

Yet even when kids know the truth, they can of course become groomed over time to expect our empty praises. Who doesn't like to hear good things about themselves? I know I do. We also fell into the "good job!" trap when our kids were little. Recently, as my daughter and I cleaned out her room and sorted through stacks upon stacks of old drawings—making piles for recycling, for her to keep, for me to keep—she was offended when I would send anything to the recycling graveyard. Sure, part of that is she knows I'm nostalgic and would save everything if I could. But another part of this whole mess is she's still used to being praised for whatever she does. For making so much as a crooked line across a piece of paper. Because we have done it, other parents have done it, her teachers have done it, our culture has done it. We are good job—ing kids right into incompetency.

When she first tried horseback riding—something that is a hobby of the rich for a reason, as we have painfully discovered—we were fortunate to find a tough teacher. She's around my age and doesn't have children. I think that part is important. And she doesn't teach a ton of kids; it's not a kid-centric farm, another key factor. She is a horse person; she takes horses seriously. She takes the care of them seriously. And she knows firsthand if you fuck around when it comes to horses, you can find yourself in a world of hurt.

My daughter was finishing up her very first attempt at tacking up her horse and Mary, her instructor, commented, "Okay, so you say you're done. Can you tell me that is absolutely the best job you can do? That animal is depending on you to do your best."

D-A-M-N. I was standing behind Mary, and my daughter and I exchanged a look like we had both been punched in the face. But that punch felt good to me. I realized as much as I thought I was trying to back away from overly praising her every breath and move, I needed to relearn what real talk was. It wasn't about breaking anyone down or being needlessly cruel. It was about introducing the concept that there are standards. That life is a process of rising up to meet those standards. That hard work is essential to building confidence and feeling capable. And, most important, there is always more to learn. We can always get better at whatever it is we do.

My daughter has slipped up only a few times since then. She has learned to be meticulous with her horse. Because she has been introduced to those expectations. And Mary isn't going to get in there and help her do it. She doesn't care that my daughter's eleven and her mom is standing right there. Not her problem. She trusts that my daughter can do it, and after feeling a bit adrift without all that supervision and hand-holding, my daughter could do it herself. She had been pushed beyond her comfort zone and rose to the challenge. Maybe it wasn't the most difficult challenge in the world, but it was one more step in what should be a lifelong journey of building competency.

And while kids deserve to experience true competition as well as discover what they are uniquely good at, it's just as valuable for them to know where and when to cut bait.

In my own experience, learning what I suck at has been just as important as identifying my strengths. It tells me what I should no longer put energy toward or beat myself up over. And it allows me to channel my focus, talent, and attention on the things that matter. It's insane to imagine an adult being equally good at acting, singing, football, playing the piano, drawing, baseball, horseback riding, coding, writing jokes, and archery. Yet this is what we're telling kids every day. You are good—no, great—at everything. Your work here is done.

There is nothing quite like that edgy and exciting feeling of trying out for something, competing, waiting to see if your name is on the list. The callback, the team, the cast. I have stood on tippy-toes on the outskirts of a huddle of teenagers scanning for my name. I have been elated. I have been crushed. Each experience taught me that the things you want don't always come easy, and sometimes they don't come at all. Sometimes it showed me that the things I thought I wanted, I actually didn't. I wanted them because my friends wanted them or someone else wanted them for me, but I just didn't have it in me. Or maybe I wanted to be good at this one particular thing but I wasn't, plain and simple. Instead of beating my head against the twin brick walls of fate and genetics, better to plow my drive and smarts into something I could actually improve in.

When we deny our kids that sort of process, to figure out their natural gifts, their potential gifts, to let go of the stuff they're just not good at so they can invest more in the areas where they show true passion and promise, we are denying them the process of growing up. Of being prepared for the world they will be living in, a world where they will get their asses handed to them on a regular basis.

Nowhere is this clash across generations and the mismatching of expectations more glaringly apparent than in the workplace. And sure, this whole "you damn kids don't know the meaning of hard work" and "you also don't know how to deal with criticism, like, at all" complaint isn't new, but watch me launch into it anyway.

I've stood speechless as interns scoffed at the tasks they'd been given as I simultaneously recalled all the months I spent standing in front of a copier with my pumps off when I was an intern. All of us of a certain age, collectively willing the cycle of professional hazing to continue, can barely contain ourselves from screaming, "You're an INTERN, JACKASS." Or junior designers who would expect to be made senior designers after surviving in their jobs for twelve whole months! All by themselves! They weren't born with those expectations; those expectations were nurtured. They went through elementary school, middle school, high school, and college being told they were excellent, talented, and without a single flaw. That they deserved things— promotions, raises, accolades—simply for showing up.

"What's wrong with kids these days?" looks a lot like how we're raising kids right now. With the golden light of perfection, always shining down upon them. We don't want them to be sad or frustrated, because that makes us feel bad. It makes us feel like terrible parents. But if that's how we're going to do things, then we should at least own the fact that when we hand out trophies and ribbons and certificates merely for existing, what we are actually saying is this—"You have won now. But you will lose so much more later."

September 17, 2010: The Day
I Turned the Car Around

There are only a handful of things I'll never forget. Most I'll never remember.

Of course I didn't know that at the time.

In those first few years of growing and feeding and burping and bouncing and cursing and loving my kids, I was saturated with experiences, bowled over by firsts, and laid low by exhaustion and frustration. Call it what you will, "The happiest time of your life" (really?), "the early days," "new motherhood," but no matter what you call it there's no denying it's vivid.

I trusted my brain to file away every favorite food and word, all the mannerisms and comedy routines, funny walks and mind-bending questions. Even though I was submerged in serious stress and suffering from a profound lack of sleep, I still felt confident the sheer novelty of these moments were enough to leave indelible marks, like bronzed fingerprints, all over my brain. I figured there was no way I could forget even a single second of it.

I remember almost none of it.

I probably forgot most of it almost as quickly as it happened. Details were swapped out for newer details, mannerisms swapped out for the latest models, foods and jokes and questions all updated with the latest version. It was as if a dialogue box kept popping up in my head that read, "An item that's similar already exists in this location. Do you want to replace it with the one that's happening right now?" and I clicked "yes" over and over again.

But there is one day that stands out. Oh, ho boy, does it.

We were setting off for a day trip to a children's science museum a solid one-hour-and-forty-five-minute drive from our house. I remember the exact drive time because it became a regular destination once my kids were old enough (and I was capable enough) to make it worthwhile. It had everything going for it. Exhibits awaited kid fingers and eyes and ears—there were gears to be cranked and buttons to be pushed, sounds to hear and sights to see. No need to have excuses at the ready for strangers! No four-and-a-half-minute preparatory speech in the car before they were released! This was a place for them and their people. There is a certain sort of disgusting relief in that. Those are the days you know you're an American mom. Those are the days you feel unnatural gratitude for whoever invented stickers and then came up with systems to use them. Those are the days you have nothing to lose.

In the summer, the museum expanded to include an out-door science park with water exhibits. I can still picture my two little sidekicks on one of our earliest trips, in swim diapers and swimsuits, chubby thighs and exploding delight as the fountains popped up and disappeared. Back inside, they made giant bubbles and totally touched the stuffed moose surrounded by DO NOT TOUCH signs and reasonable explanations of why not (oils from your hands, old fur, something something, I really don't remember). There were penny games, miniature tornadoes, and contained fog, and an indoor play area with tunnels and a tower for the youngest kids. That place was perfect. No matter what, by the time we left they'd be tuckered out and happy. And I'd have the satisfaction of feeling like we had done something educational even if all they got out of it was the incontrovertible fact that leaf-cutting ants are a one-way ticket to Heebie-Jeebie-ville.

After one last trip to the bathroom they'd be in clean, dry clothes, with full bellies from a late lunch, imaginations tweaked, and tired legs from exploring. I'd buckle them back into the car, feeling happy we had had a full day out in the world. It's still surprising to me how gratifying it can be to simply check off those basics, to feel like I've provided them with simple comforts and a little joy.

But before I get too misty-eyed about it, the other thing that was gratifying about that trip was—without fail—they'd both completely crash out either on the way there or back. So to sum up: guaranteed quiet time, ability to listen to NPR like the good liberal bubble-dweller that I am, boundless opportunity to drink my coffee in orgasmic peace while also escaping the natural disaster that was our house? Obviously add me to your mailing list, science nerds. Of course I'll join your museum. *Take all my money.*

I'm not going to be modest about this: September 17, 2010, still stands as the single best day in my parenting history.

Our morning started out as so many others had—a loose plan, a patriotic amount of snacks packed, coffee in hand, and fully ready to feel the glory of the open road. Let's get the hell out of this house and out into the world, kids. We've got people to irritate! And like so many other mornings, there was a whole lot of repeating of instructions and not listening and it taking us as much time to get out the door as it would have to drive all the way there already. They were fighting and foot dragging and working my last nerve, but I didn't see those as signs of things to come, I just saw those as signs that we were all awake.

We broke the surly bonds of our driveway and then our street, our neighborhood, then that other neighborhood and a few more, finally gliding onto the interstate—nothing but super-sexy highway as far as the eye could see. Initiate driving sequence: Coffee being ingested? Check. NPR on? Check. Kids quietly relaxing in the back seat, not at all sticking their fingers into each other's armpits, tummies, eyes, and/or ears? Negative. Houston, we have a cliché. This was not the blastoff I was hoping for.

That day was overcast after a storm and puddles of sloshy, muddy water dotted sidewalks and roads. My kids were still relatively little—four and six—but certainly the proverbial "old enough to know better" on so many levels. They more or less understood rules, they pretty much knew what would get them into trouble, they mostly listened to me, and I *thought* they understood what would send curtains of hellfire raining down upon their heads, but clearly I was mistaken.

It hadn't even been a half hour before it became clear it was still bullshit o'clock in my car in a big way. They didn't listen. When I asked them to stop, they did the straight-up opposite of the words that were coming out of my face. Their expressions told me over and over again, "Oh we heard you. We just really don't seem to care about what you're saying at this particular moment." Undaunted, and having already invested entirely too much time and effort in our jailhouse break, there was no way in hell we were turning back now. OR WERE WE.

Why were these children who I loved so very much trying to rob me of *my* simple joys? This was my chill time, my you-guys-shut-up-and-I-listen-to-NPR time, and they were totally ruining it. It also became clear that "I went to the bathroom before we left" was the biggest lie that had ever been lied and we were already pulling off at a rest area.

Much unbuckling and holding of hands ensued. The whole

performative dance that is little kids and a mom in a rest-area bathroom commenced. My son was terrified of loud sounds and hadn't yet mastered the one-arm-wrap-around-cover-both-ears move that would become his signature later. So he shuffled in with hands mashed over his head, wary of the hand dryers that were going off as all the callous adult hand washers went about their business, blasting those things left and right. He had no hands free to actually undo his pants and pull down his under-pants. So that was definitely one of my favorite arguments we always got in, the one about needing your hands.

"NO, I'M NOT MOVING MY HANDS."

"YOU NEED YOUR HANDS."

"NO, IT'S TOO LOUD."

"BUT HANDS" and on and on until I keel over dead.

Whenever we would actually survive the hand-dryer assault, it'd be on to the horror of spontaneously flushing toilets that would send both kids over the edge. In all fairness, if there's one thing that should be predictable in its behavior, it's a toilet. No-body needs to be naked from hips to knees and shift their weight ever so slightly only to be greeted with a random spritz of toilet water up the ol' caboose while simultaneously feeling like maybe you'll be sucked down into the center of the earth.

Mercifully fleeing the Tasmanian vortex in the bathroom stall, it'd be off to the sink to wash hands, which, again, is hard to do when you don't use your actual hands because they're slammed against your ears as prep for the HAND-DRYER RE-MATCH. OH MY GOD.

After what easily felt like five days, we were finally free of the bathrooms. I beelined for the car, wiping my dripping-wet hands on my jeans and thinking, did I ever really used to enter, use, and exit the bathroom in under a week in my previous life? I feel like I did. I mean, I must have. As my brain was caught up in trying to solve this life puzzle, I whipped around to make sure my kids were actually still following me.

That's when I saw them, just as they spied the muddy puddles. They heard me say, "DON'T JUMP IN THOSE MUDDY PUDDLES!" and "SERIOUSLY DO. NOT. YOU DON'T HAVE ANY CLEAN—" and there they went. Jumping and giggling, with that glint in their eyes that said, "LOL PARENTING."

Typically in this sort of situation I would resort to the time-honored parenting method commonly referred to as "losing one's shit," which is largely associated with actions that include but are not limited to yelling and counting slowly and loudly up to three. But I had recently discovered when things got especially dark, it was more effective if I took a different tack. With what I imagined to be the sort of approach the Mafia might employ, I pulled both kids close to me, put my lips right to their ears, and in a voice so disturbingly quiet they could barely hear me, I hissed, "*get. in the car. now.*"

Why this works, I have no idea. It still works. To be fair, I think if someone came up to me, clasped my head, and whispered something mildly threatening I would definitely do whatever they said. Even let them take me to the second location. Whatever. I would just want the arm or head clasping and the intimate weird whispering to end.

As I ushered them along through the sheer force of my cumulative anger I announced, "This is your last warning. If you guys don't listen and keep getting in trouble, we're going home. Do you hear me?"

How many times have we all said something like that? I'd also accept other variations on this theme like, "Do you want to leave now?" "Should we go home now?" "That's it, we're going home now." "This is your final warning." "I'm not saying it one more time." "This is the last time I say it." "Did you hear me say this is the last time I'm going to say it?" "Okay I'll say it one more time, this is it." And "I mean it this time."

There's really nothing like saying, "That's the last time I'm going to say it" to boldly underline how much it really is *not* the last time you're going to say it. What we're all basically saying, over and over again, is, "I do not want to go through the physical effort—never mind the behavioral shit storm—that will be unleashed if I try to put this whole thing in motion." And as we all know, it's even more meaningless when we're threatening to leave a thing or place where we as parents actually want to stay. The beach, a movie, a party, anywhere that's not our own house. That's when the threats are as hollow as my soul.

Eventually we all returned to the car, me fuming and feeling the weight of this "final warning" now hanging over me, them only the slightest bit delayed, as if they had hit a speed bump going twenty-seven instead of the suggested twenty-five. I eased the car back onto the highway, turned the radio up, and hoped that was the end of it.

After what was maybe a fifteen-minute reprieve tops—during which I imagine they had unfurled an old-timey map across their laps to hash out their battle plan like little World War II generals—they started fighting again. And harassing each other. And screaming and yelling. Which caused me to scream and yell back and tell them to knock it off because they had already had one warning—DIDN'T THEY REMEMBER THAT? IT WAS THE LAST ONE. THE LAST ONE BEFORE THE ONE I JUST SAID.

And that's when it happened. Of course, like so many other things, the details of what exactly that last straw was remain lost to history. It might've been a smack or a slap or a poke or a scream or them calling each other "a butt," who knows. All I know is that it was enough for me to see an exit coming up, put on my turn signal, and in a remarkably calm voice say, "That's it."

LIGHTNING.

"I warned you guys."

THUNDER.

My car took the exit.

THE STORM IS CLOSER THAN YOU THINK.

Both kids immediately erupted in screams as my car took the off ramp, hooked a left, continued across the overpass, and then got back on the highway—in the opposite direction.

"NO, MOM, NO NO NO!" I had never heard them simultaneously scream and beg so loudly in my entire life. My ears were ringing. If the windows had been down, anyone passing us couldn't be blamed if they thought a crime was being committed in my vehicle.

Neither my husband nor I had ever pulled off such a day-obliterating move before. They didn't know whether to cry or shriek or beg or completely flip out, so they did all those things at the same time. BOTH KIDS DID ALL THOSE THINGS AT THE SAME TIME.

They were hysterical; they could not be contained. They were thrashing around, begging for mercy. They were crying so hard they couldn't even breathe, one of them started coughing and choking. They kept triggering each other exponentially with their freak-outs, because as much as one kid was freaking out, seeing their sibling freak out at this never-before-seen freak-out level was sending both of them spiraling into the freak-out stratosphere. They begged for one more chance: *"Please please please, Mom."* They promised to be good for the rest of the drive, for the whole day, for the rest of their lives.

"Nope, too late. We're going home."

AAAAAHHHHHHHHHHHHHHHHHHHHHHHHHHHHHH!!!
Another wave of pure psychological breakdown engulfed the car. They had just learned the world was a real fuck show of a place and other people can destroy your damn lives, *just like that.* Even people who you had previously trusted and thought you loved. And those people could do it without flinching. Without feeling sorry about it. All while sipping their coffee.

I turned the radio up. I felt so . . . calm. One might even say peaceful. I had a slight grin that wouldn't have been out of place on the face of a serial killer. The screaming and begging continued. I turned the radio up a little louder. It's really hard to hear the latest in national and local news, not to mention the seventeen-minute-long weather report, with all that screaming and carrying on.

After what felt like infinity minutes of this rolling horror show, I pulled off the highway to send my husband a text. The kids took this as a sign that I might turn the car back around. An eerie silence settled over us. They realized I was capable of anything now.

I typed, "We were an hour and fifteen minutes into our drive to Montshire. We were less than a half hour away. The kids were acting like dicks. I just turned the car around. It feels good. It feels timeless."

Send.

My kids are now eleven and thirteen. To this day, that's the only time I ever turned the car around. It was the only time I've had to. That one spontaneous decision blossomed into a long-term investment. I never had to tell them I'd pull some serious shit if they were misbehaving, because they had already seen me do it up close.

All I had to say was, "Do you really want to try me?" and turns out they didn't. They knew. Of course, they were little then. And we're hardly into the wilds of the teenage years now, a time when I won't expect more than a shrug even if I dynamited our entire house. But it was a good run.

So do it. Turn the car around. Leave the party. Blow up the movie plans. Kill the beach trip. Carry them out over your shoulder kicking and screaming and, yes, in public. You're the one in charge. It feels good to remember that part. Just one suggestion from a veteran of September 17—only throw that threat down for something you really don't care about missing. Because who are you really trying to punish anyway?

The Ghosts of Halloweens Past

I walked past a towering barn and through the late-autumn woods; stubborn yellow leaves the only ones left hanging on to stark, alarmed branches. Sunflower stalks arched into canes, their heads bowed in grief. The smell of the forest in the fall is unmistakable, all of that decaying earthy sweetness underfoot. I feel wrapped in comfort and loss, time slipping away. The wind choosing to lie very still, holding its breath, or blow up in a huff, causing me to feel panic down to my toes.

Shuffling through the leaves and somber air sent me back to the fall days I took for granted when I was growing up in my small hometown in Massachusetts. Taking things for granted was my specialty back then, when I was a kid and then a teenager. If I were to pause long enough I'd realize it still is.

Halloween isn't until this weekend and, as is customary now, my kids have already celebrated it twice. I had to think back to what costumes I used to wear, when Halloween came just once. I don't remember my parents being involved at all, although they must have been. For at least two Halloweens I dressed up like a hobo, the go-to costume for the unprepared— although with my flannel shirt, bandanna tied to a stick, rosy-red checks and straw hat, I looked more like a cross between a scarecrow and a rodeo clown. My friend Linda and I made a plan, put on our costumes, and went trick-or-treating. Alone. Parents didn't tag along then, and they certainly didn't make it

an occasion for walking around the neighborhood with cocktails.

Now after more than ten years of parenting-while-under-
the-influence-of-Halloween, it's had its effect. There are always
costumes to get, details to nail down, trick-or-treating to arrange,
maybe a class party to contribute to. I skate on the very edge of
helpfulness generally speaking, and yet, it still happens. I still end
up in the mix. I want my kids to have fun, and I want to take
pictures. I'm convinced "I wanted my kids to have fun" will be
etched on the vast majority of modern mothers' tombstones. And
"She wanted to take pictures" is what kids will request on theirs.

But Halloween is beginning to feel smaller. Although my
son plans on wearing the same police officer costume he's worn
for the past four years, he hesitated when we attended a Halloween parade over the weekend. Never mind that he's worn it
year-round to ride his bike or give visitors a tour of our house,
suddenly at an actual Halloween-themed event he balked. "I
feel like a jerk" was the first thing he said when we arrived, even
though kids his age as well as teenagers and adults were also in
costume. This is the year he's noticing differences and other kids
are noticing what's different about him. And although I know
he's not the only one going through this, he does not.

My daughter decided to go as an artist this year, and she
gave me a very specific list of the wardrobe items she hoped for. I
kept badgering her to add a beret and make a painter's palette so,
you know, people would know what she actually was. She stuck
to her list. By some sort of thrifting miracle, I found every single
item during a twenty-minute sweep of Goodwill. I even found a
black beret and bought it, knowing she'd probably refuse it. And
she did. And I was done with Halloween prep, just like that.

When they were younger I would question them throughout
September about what they wanted to be. Once I managed to

get three consistent answers in a row, I'd start scouring eBay and Etsy for costumes. A unicorn, a puppy, a skunk, and a black cat have all arrived in the mail. A third of the costumes handmade by someone else, the sweetest of scores. Improbably, one year I tracked down a bluebird costume. ("Are you sure you don't want to be a peacock? Those are easier for me to find.") Someone had made it by stitching a blue feather boa all over a blue Old Navy sweatshirt in a size just big enough for my daughter. In the package were the matching yellow feet that could be threaded through her shoelaces and a beak to go over her nose.

As they've gotten older, I've slowly come to realize that Halloween—like first days of school and believing in Santa—doesn't actually go on forever. That every exasperated "Ugh, I can't wait for Halloween to be over" as I scrambled to the store to get face paint or nail polish or tights, is now being met with the realization that someday it will be over. For good. Relief. Then, regret.

I would've trick or treated until I left for college if my parents had let me, but my dad took me off the candy-shakedown circuit when I was thirteen. And just like that, instead of raking in free Snickers at the whopping nine houses on our dead-end street, I ended up in a soccer field in the dark with my girlfriends and boys who were two or three years older than us. We had eggs cracked on our heads and maple syrup poured on our letterman jackets. We slid down hills near the soccer field in the dark and ran around screaming.

It felt, in that any-attention-is-good-attention way, like a baptism. I wasn't a kid anymore; I was a teenager, a troublemaker. Someone who would walk into her small-town grocery store, smeared with what was essentially half a recipe, and walk nonchalantly to the refrigerated section to grab as many cartons of eggs as I had cash. It was the kind of night where you stand with your best friend in line, knowing your life is changing but not sure exactly how, and say too loudly to each other as you pay for all those eggs, "Oh man, can't wait to bake a REALLY BIG CAKE when we get home" as if those cashiers had the intelligence of a pile of rocks with eyes. As if they had never been young.

The long arching branches that bow over the paths I've walked, the crisp leaves I've kicked through, and the dirt roads I've driven down since returning to New England all call me back to other high school parties held among the hay bales and in distant fields. Nights when we hung upside down from branches in a graveyard, smoking cigarettes and screaming just to hear our own voices. Couples kissing next to tombstones, lying on long-ago repacked dirt, their outstretched bodies just feet above skeletons, the taste of peppermint schnapps on their lips. I can still feel the sharp October air of those nights and see the face of the full moon, watching us live among the dead.

But times change. Towns barely allow actual trick-or-treating anymore, never mind egg massacres and graveyard parties. Some things never change though, like outgrowing who you were before. It happens when you're nine and eleven and, as it turns out, forty-seven. You feel different and you know things are different, but you're not sure how. Like a toddler straight out of an attachment-parenting book, you rush ahead but keep checking back in. My kids check back in with me now as intensely as they want to take off without me. I stumble out into whatever this next phase of my life is, and I check back in with them too. Are we still us?

I know the real Halloweens—the ones made for kid costumes and candy trading—aren't over, not really, not yet. But it's like seeing the leaves change on that first tree in August. The one that just can't hold its horses. My kids are racing into life. A life that one day will go on without me.

As Halloween approached, I told my daughter in a last-ditch effort, "But if people see the beret, they'll know you're an artist." She shook her head and said, "I'll know I'm an artist." And having known a lot of artists, I can verify not one of them has ever worn a beret but a lot of them have worn knee-high boots, a shirt splattered with paint, or bright colors in their hair, just like she planned on wearing.

Every day they're trying on who they want to be. I see them gauging reactions, measuring laughs, reluctantly accepting hugs and kisses on cheeks. They grow their hair long; she asks to get her ears pierced or wear makeup; he flashes a peace sign at his friends on the bus as it rolls away. They feel the shift of their own strange baptisms already and the pull of attention.

I've reached back, through the smell of woodsmoke and the opening of milkweed, to realize I was once a child in autumn too. I have roamed neighborhoods and forests and graveyards, feeling invincible. Immortal. I have hesitated and balked, then run full force into the unknown.

It's their time now. To try on and try out. To forge their own paths through these shifting seasons. The rituals we created together will inevitably wane; they will have to. It is the wide-open field, begging for exploration, and the cold blue sky pointing the way toward migration. It is the flat, still air and the sudden huffing and puffing of change.

TIME-OUT

Radiohead Song or Accurate Description of My Parenting?

1. Scatterbrain
2. Arbitrary Justice
3. I Might Be Wrong
4. Slammed Doors
5. 2 + 2 = 5
6. Go to Sleep
7. I Can't
8. Head in Hands
9. Down Is the New Up
10. Existential Implosion
11. Sulk
12. Stop Whispering
13. Dirty Laundry Infinity
14. Shouting Out of Proportion
15. Let Down
16. I Told You a Thousand Times
17. You and Whose Army?
18. Man Down
19. Slips of Permission
20. Fog
21. Life in a Glass House
22. Who's the Adult?

23. Worrywort
24. You Never Wash Up After Yourself
25. Red Wine Massacre
26. 4 Minute Warning
27. Crying in Public
28. These Are My Twisted Words
29. A Reminder
30. I Never Said I Knew What I Was Doing
31. House of Cards
32. At a Loss
33. I Am Citizen Insane
34. Accidental Successes
35. Permanent Daylight
36. What

Radiohead song: 1, 6, 7, 9, 11, 12, 17, 20, 21, 24, 26, 28, 29, 31, 35
Accurate description of my parenting: 2, 4, 8, 10, 13, 14, 16, 18, 19, 22, 25, 27, 30, 32, 34, 36
Both: 3, 5, 15, 23, 33

Are You Sure There Isn't Something Else I Can Do Before the End of the School Year?

Are you sure I can't fill out and/or sign another field-trip form / fund-raising form / class placement form / book-order form / class-party form / Popsicle request / overdue-library-books notice / missing-library-books notice / school-district-feedback form / one month of half-filled-out reading logs?

Are you sure I can't contribute to one last bake sale, or five? Are you sure I can't make it something gluten-free, nut-free, egg-free, dairy-free, non-GMO, organic, and/or won't hurt anyone's feelings? Are you sure bright pink fake-fat frosting from a can won't work? Have I mentioned I have the culinary skills of a potato?

Are you sure I can't send in money for a yearbook? A class trip to get ice cream sandwiches? A PTO donation? A visiting author's signed book? Tickets for the end-of-school-year party? A baseball game? The stupid recorders I didn't even want my kids to have in the first place?

Are you sure I can't get the money to you in the form of a check because I'm a pioneer woman? Are you positive you don't want to accept PayPal or Square or— No, I know. That's crazy. You're not a spaceship.

Are you sure I can't chaperone one or all eleven of the field trips between now and the last day of school? Don't worry, I no longer have time to hold down a job. By the way, remember all that time between January and April? What happened there?

Are you sure there isn't some sort of spring concert / adorable play / other emotionally manipulative school event to go to now or every night until the last day of school? You know, something where maybe one of the boys can wear a too-big tie or the tallest girl in class can shyly stoop down in the back row? Maybe it could be a third-grade dance or a fifth-grade graduation? That sort of thing.

Are you sure 273 art projects couldn't be sent home all at once? Preferably stuffed into a flimsy about-to-split-open plastic grocery bag? Are you sure you aren't giving me some other kid's stuff too?

Are you sure there can't be some sort of complicated theme weeks my kids can get all whipped up over even though they could barely manage to pair a shirt with pants the other forty-one weeks of the year? If possible, could it be something where we'll have to gather an incredibly random assortment of props on extremely short notice? Maybe an orange wig, two different colors of the same style of shoes, and a sports jersey from 1991? Just spitballing here. Can you make sure any errands related to each theme can be spread out among multiple locations across town thereby obliterating one entire day from the scoreboard of my life?

Are you sure a room parent can't come up with one or three end-of-year classroom projects like that one time when we had two days' notice for each kid to cut out thirty-eight two-inch-by-two-inch squares for a paper mosaic project? And I mean two inches by two inches exactly; it said so in the e-mail. Something complicated and requiring extreme precision is exactly the sort of thing I'm in the mood for right now. Got anything like that?

Are you sure I can't get you a teacher gift? Are you sure I

can't read some shitty mom blog posts about what an appropriate teacher gift might be? Are you sure I can't just get you a nice bottle of wine? I have one right here; it's already open.

Are you sure you need to give me that summer reading list / library flyer / academic camp brochure? Are you sure I can't just let my kids get dumber by one-third until they come back here in the fall like we all used to?

Are you sure you can't make me panic more about how little time I have until the school year is almost over? So I can be reminded the only thing that allows me to approach my work with any sort of mental and structural stability (not to mention without going bankrupt, ha!) is about to go away for ten weeks? I'm not panicking enough about that. Can you help me?

SCHOOLS

The Walls That Define Us

I showed up to my son's kindergarten tour same-day hungover.
Because as it turned out, it was also the day I lost my job of six
years. The job we had moved across the country for. I never saw
it coming.

Mostly what I remember about that night — aside from the
deep existential panic, throbbing headache, and the fact I was
grateful I didn't know anyone because maybe my face was always this splotchy and my eyes always this bloodshot? — was seeing all the artwork on the walls as we walked around. I wasn't
sure when I had last been inside an elementary school, but it was
an amount of time measured in decades.

The art-filled bulletin boards swooped me back to my favorite elementary school teacher, Miss Slozak, who indulged my ob-
session with Snoopy by letting me draw him over and over again
for her classroom walls. I reflexively smiled at the self-portraits
bursting with Chiclet teeth and spider-lashed eyes, yarn hair
and names carefully written out in blocky letters. I eventually fell
behind our small tour group, staring at a papier-mâché solar system through increasingly tear-blurred eyes and wondered, *Will
my son even go here? Will we have to move? Have I let everyone
down?*

But we stayed, I started freelancing two days later, and he
went to that school — Vermont's first arts magnet elementary
school — and so did his sister. What had been a failing school

in a poor neighborhood was entering a transition period of becoming something different, something greater. And, I hoped, so were we.

What struck me every morning I walked through those doors and every afternoon as I lingered, waiting for the bell to ring, were those walls. A construction-paper pumpkin patch with a Van Gogh sky. Family portraits and abstract trees, windows covered with tissue-paper stained glass and a hallway populated with kraft-paper penguin families, made to scale. And while it was an arts-focused school, every elementary school was supposed to feel like this. Learning and creativity made visible, a safe place to wear your heart on the outside.

But it seems life is never that simple, not always what the brochure promises. My son had a slow-motion train wreck of a kindergarten year, where I heard about his horrible day almost every day, how he crawled under tables crying, clapped his hands over his ears and shook, his behaviors new and awful. His school not knowing how to parse a bright boy with unpredictable freak-outs.

In one memorable meeting, I watched politics play out between the principal, teachers, and the special ed staff while my temper slowly rose like a cartoon thermometer. My son discussed as a problem that didn't fit neatly into their process. I sat there bewildered and on the edge of tears, finally hissing, "Why won't you *help him*?" If a public elementary school wouldn't help my kid, I reasoned, who would? Aren't these the schools for everyone? For every child? No matter what?

For every valley, there was a peak. A new principal was eventually hired — and, most important, stayed. This school we took a chance on took chances on us over and over again, even as we left for a year to homeschool and worked hard to get him to a place where he could reenroll. He found his champions every single year and with a depth of gratitude I'll feel for the rest of my life—they found him too.

My daughter found her own favorite teacher, one who indulged her with an entire day in her honor before we moved to another town. She stoked her kindness, kept her eye on the already complex labyrinth of girl friendships in her class, and challenged my daughter with a firm hand and loads of love.

I've sat through talent shows that lasted three and a half hours too long, downed a medicating glass of wine before every school Halloween party, and felt unabashedly hopeful about the world listening to tentative voices pipe up at winter concerts.

I have felt a part of something, buoyed.

I have also watched children dragged and shoved into school by parents barely tethered to earth. My husband took our son to his best friend's house for her sixth birthday party only to find used needles scattered around the yard, drunk adults filling up the apartment. I have seen kids showing up to school with just a soda for breakfast or without a coat in the middle of a Vermont winter.

I raced to the regular all-school Friday assembly on the afternoon of December 14, 2012, just hours after the Sandy Hook shooting. Our principal led the kids through the most normal-seeming town hall meeting while parents looked at each other with pleading, shattered eyes. We longed for it to be over so we could rush to our sons and daughters, to hug them too hard, stick our noses in their hair, and wonder at their physicality, their presence. Every glance around the room as we waited for that moment—every pair of eyes meeting—serving as silent confirmation that, yes, it had happened, it was real. These were kids our kids' ages. Their school, their teachers, their paras, not unlike our school, our teachers, our paras.

I have felt broken.

I used to think of elementary school as a place for my children to learn, to become more of who they are. What I hadn't anticipated is that I have become more of who I am too.

My daughter's passionate and almost obsessive love for her friends — regardless of how they treated her or whether they returned those feelings — has mirrored my own struggles with friendship. What parenting books don't prepare you for are the conversations you will have with your soft-cheeked daughter, the one who is cheerful and loving and just a straight-up kick in the pants, as you teach her how to harden her heart.

Within these walls I have made and lost my own friends — both in spectacular fashion. I have stood alongside them as we cackled at inside jokes or locked eyes across the gym as we cried with joy over a performance. And then, after everything fell apart, I struggled to understand where I fit in. Instead of constantly claiming what my kids got from me, the past eight years have been a slow revealing of things I didn't know were inside of me, apart from them.

In just two weeks our family will be done with elementary school. Not for the school year, but forever. This fact only hitting me straight between the eyes days ago. Maybe because my daughter's prep for middle school has mirrored her prep for kindergarten — she was born ready and we are left trying to keep up.

I've sat stunned in random five-minute grabs of silence realizing that, much like trying to get a good night's sleep or suffering through potty training, I just thought we'd always be parents of young kids. They would be this age, this size, this digging-in-the-dirt, picking-flowers, needing-me, needing-us way forever. They would just always be in elementary school.

Yet forevers come to a close all the time. They certainly come to a close every June.

Last fall when I picked up my son from his first middle school dance, I again fell down a rabbit hole of nostalgia, much like I had on that first elementary school tour. But it was different. Because within those walls and that post-dance stink, girls on their phones and boys flipping water bottles, it felt like the beginning of moving away. Those walls were different, full of trophies and dance banners, news of elections and photos of volunteering. Those were the walls of becoming who he is, away from us.

I realize I am hopelessly bound by the mythology of this country, that I am supposed to make it all on my own, pulling myself up by my bootstraps every step of the way. Maybe that's why elementary school feels sacred; it's the one place where I — as a child, as a parent — have been allowed to feel vulnerable, cared for, safe. Every violation of that relentlessly hopeful assumption, from bullying to lunch shaming, fills me with inexplicable sadness and rage.

I am offended at the breach.

These walls, these art-dotted walls, represent a promise — a promise that others will see you, they will see if you are hungry, if you are struggling, if you are broken. They will see the best of you, the potential in you, because it is far too early to give up. They will tell you this is a place where it's okay to cry or shout out with surprise, to throw snowballs at recess and pick tiny tomatoes from the garden just at the edges of the playground. This is a place where you are wanted and where you belong. And this is a place where parents can roam the halls before these years have even begun, and again as they come to a close, their eyes swelling with tears over the fast-forward slow motion of time.

Pro/Con: Caving to
PTO Bake Sale Pressure

PRO: Finally doing something for my kids' school.
CON: Don't want to do anything for my kids' school.

PRO: Was already going to hell anyway.
CON: Don't love the heat.

PRO: Will see a lot of familiar faces.
CON: Will remind me of the oven I'm currently avoiding.

PRO: Could always just go buy something at the market and rough it up a little.
CON: They said it had to be homemade. And they're expert level at sniffing out homemade-baked-goods fraud.

PRO: I'm expert level at choosing the easiest thing to bake.
CON: I'm non–expert level at following basic package instructions a monkey could master.

PRO: Was always curious what monkeys were better at than me. Now I know.
CON: No monkeys available in neighborhood to outsource this to.

PRO: Thinking about monkeys.
CON: . . .

PRO: Skim the crappiest brownies for myself.
CON: They're really crappy.

PRO: They're still brownies.
CON: Self-loathing.

PRO: Hero to my kids when they smell fresh-baked brownies as they walk in the door after school.
CON: I already brought the brownies to school.

PRO: Except the ones I didn't.
CON: And those brownies are long gone, too, suckas.

PRO: "But they benefit your school."
CON: *(whispers to self)* "And my desire to eat brownies in secret."

PRO: Important life lesson about how harsh the world can be.
CON: Especially the part of the world that's our kitchen.

PRO: I'm not here to make friends.
CON: So far succeeding.

PRO: Could respond to future PTO requests with "NEW E-MAIL, WHO DIS?"
CON: They'll know it's me.

PRO: Willing to jump on that grenade.
CON: Talk of grenades frowned upon at school.

PRO: It's a figure of speech.
CON: No shit, Sherlock.

PRO: Fighting with myself in list form is still better than making something for the bake sale.
CON: You don't get secret brownies from fighting with yourself in list form.

PRO: But you don't have to bake anything either.
CON: Homeschool.

The Punching Season

Some people are smart about where they choose to live. Some people live in places where they can walk outside in February and still feel their extremities. Some people live in places where three layers of pants aren't required to take the dog out for a walk and their kids don't have to dress like members of Pussy Riot just to catch the school bus. Some people are smart like that. I am not some people.

If you don't live where it snows for keeps or where the cheerfully named "wintry mix" can ruin everyone's life or where sub-zero days stack up like hash marks on a prison wall, you might not have experienced the very dark night of the soul that is late February and early March in Vermont. The excitement your family felt about a white Christmas, snowmen, and sleigh rides feels like a story you were told a hundred years ago. You truly believe you'll never see a flower that grows in the ground again and you wonder, for the twelfth winter in a row, why you choose to live in such a godforsaken place. From your nest of misery you scroll through photos from the previous summer to convince yourself it was warm once so maybe it will be again. The merciful winter amnesia that will wipe these dark days from your memory the minute a single blade of grass pops up is still a fistful of weeks away. You measure everything in fists now. Because this right here? It's the Punching Season.

And then: the colds hit. And not just the colds, but the

stomach bugs that usher in storm fronts of throwing up, diarrhea, and a desire to single-handedly destroy the earth. You start to wonder if maybe you angered an ancient god at some point but it slipped your mind. Let's face it: you are more forgetful these days. And there has to be some sort of explanation for this infinite hell. The flu and nonspecific horrible coughs descend upon you, your family, and engulf surrounding communities, causing you all to google things like *Child + hacking cough + when to go to the ER + real estate + Dominican Republic.*

And so it went a couple of weeks ago. When one sick kid turned into two sick kids and one very sick adult. When one sick day for me turned into seven. And when every routine we had was detonated so hard I can't believe Antonio Banderas wasn't seen striding out of them. We just tried to get through each day as best we could without crying.

Most of those days I couldn't have gotten off the couch if someone had been running in front of me with a flourless chocolate cake (why skimp, do you want me to move or what?) while someone else chased me with fire. So on the mornings the kids were feeling well enough to go to school, my husband told them in no uncertain terms they were on their own. He was leaving for work and they needed to get themselves fed, ready, and out the door on time.

As I drifted in and out of let's-call-it-sleep, I noticed the glaring absence of my commands, incessant reminders, and questions about whether they remembered how a clock worked. In their place were the sounds of my kids actually speaking to each other—chatting even—and the clattering of them clearing their spots, the crinkling of papers being stuffed into backpacks, and the rustle of snow pants and puffy coats being pulled on. As I tried to unstick my eyes long enough to check the time, my son materialized above me, leaned over, and smiled, then kissed me lightly on the forehead. The most touching and surprising of role reversals. And they were both out the door. Early.

Being jerked out of my routine and having a completely new one thrust upon us made me see how competent, how grown-up, my kids had become. Although I knew that at eight and ten they certainly didn't need my help getting dressed or eating or being walked to the end of the driveway, it was the first time I realized that although I was sinking, the ship wasn't going to go down with me. Not this time. It was a relief. And it was a little lonely, too. I had been training my replacements all along.

We need to be needed. Parenting demonstrates that in stark relief. You need us; you need us; you need us. We hate it; we love it. We are exhausted by it; we crave it. And although it took having kids for me to see it, it's of course true for everyone, throughout our lives, whether we have children or not. We each want a place in another's life. We want to know we fulfill some sort of purpose no one else possibly could. We want to be important, even if just in the moment, to this one person, in this one specific way.

The running joke about my grandmother was if you left her alone for more than twenty seconds, you'd find her ironing your dresses, your tea towels, your nicest shirts. I look back now and see that simple task—among the dozens she regularly performed— made her feel necessary. She moved the lives of those she loved forward. What may have started out as a duty, over a lifetime became a pleasure. Perhaps the greatest accomplishment any of us will have is moving the lives of those we love forward.

The following day my daughter stayed home and I felt steady enough to bolt myself to a chair and attempt to work. She took a long hot bath, ate a piece of cinnamon toast, traced *L-O-V-E-!* into the palm of my hand with her soft fingertip, and broke open a quilling kit she received for Christmas two years before. Our house was peaceful, quiet. The day unfolded as if we were at a spiritual retreat rather than in a self-imposed germ-soaked quarantine.

The next day she excitedly returned to school and my son, who had kissed me goodbye so gently and cheerfully the morning before, had come home early that same afternoon with a fever and chills. I spent the day curled up on the couch, finally able to focus on printed words long enough to read. He joined me and we lay facing each other, two coughing bookends sharing one big blue and white zigzaggy blanket. The icy sun streamed in, and we blocked our books from it with cement-gray pillows set against the window. We were a fort of sickness, reading and leaning, our legs almost the same length. I could've stayed exactly like that, sickness and all, until the first tentative days of spring. I could've stayed exactly like that forever.

I don't remember having a lot of sick days when I was growing up, certainly not as many as kids have now. I guess kids just get more of everything these days, including attention and viruses. But the sick days I did have stood out like holidays. No school. Lots of lounging. Unlimited TV. I particularly remember the afternoon my dad came home early from work carrying a fresh stack of magazines. *TigerBeat* and *Seventeen* were right on the top, that's what I remember most. I like to picture him in his business suit going into the store and browsing the particular section where these magazines were found. I try to imagine the looks. I try to imagine the reactions when he went to check out. Then again, it was the 1970s. Did people even have reactions back then?

I had a hard time swallowing pills, and to this day I can still call up what ground-up aspirin stirred into chocolate ice cream tastes like. The things we do for each other, the small gestures that tumble out of us so much more readily when we're simply given the opening. On a daily basis I will refuse to do things my kids can do for themselves and even some they can't, but there is no independence in virus-infested foxholes. I have slept on the couch as my daughter curled into a sleeping bag, our trusty blue barf bucket at the ready. I have cleaned bushels of sheets and scooped up and wiped down floors covered with such a range of disgusting fluids and, well, solids—miraculously not gagging myself—that I wonder what sort of anti-nausea superpowers I was gifted with at their births. I also wonder if it is trademarked or patented yet, and if not, how do I go about doing that? I have held hair back while breathing through my mouth and attempting to block the sound of vomiting from reaching my ears through sheer mental will. I have made mountains of cinnamon toast and rubbed miles of backs. I have admired the beautifully stained lips that come from cherry Popsicles and think makeup artists with kids must get some of their ideas from days like these. And I have upheld revered traditions: No school. Lots of lounging. Unlimited TV.

I hope when my kids are grown they'll remember even a little bit about that week. I'm sure their sick days and weeks will blur together, there have been so many. I have forgotten entire family vacations from my childhood, so maybe it's unrealistic to think they'll remember even a fraction of these days that were already hazy to begin with. But maybe they'll remember being able to stay home with me. Or the time I didn't move from our couch for an entire week. Or the baths they took, the Popsicles they ate for breakfast, lunch, and dinner. Maybe they'll remember the small actions—the cool cloth, the sip of water, the midday nap—that made a difference in how they felt.

I know I'll remember how we found an unlikely oasis during the hardest time of the year; when we felt our worst, they showed me their best, and for those quiet and adrift moments, we were a fortress of independence and interdependence.

I will remember we still had one another.

Please Don't Get Murdered at School Today

Do you have everything? Homework? Lunch? Field-trip money? I love you.

I remember one of the Sandy Hook parents said they took comfort in the fact that they had seen their child off to school that morning—you know, that morning—and said, "I love you." So before their first grader was gunned down in her classroom, she knew she was loved. I bet they all did though.

But just in case, I love you.

We've talked about all kinds of scary things, like I've told you never to get into a car with anyone you don't know and don't ever believe an adult needs your help finding a puppy or a kitten. Also: no one will ever give you a free iPad or Legos from their car, that's just not how the world works.

But for some reason, amid the talk of stranger danger and pedophiles, cancer and dying, and me sheepishly asking your friends' parents if they have a gun in the house, we haven't really talked about one of the scariest things of all. Those lockdown drills you're always having at school? No one's being straight with you about those. They're to prepare you in case someone decides to come into your school and murder you, your friends, your principal, the secretaries, and teachers before killing himself (it's pretty much always a him). Sorry about that.

I love you.

I know that may sound scary, but what you need to remember is this country was founded on freedom. And that includes the freedom of all people (sane, crazy, whatever) to have unchallenged access to guns that are capable of executing at least twenty first graders or twelve moviegoers or nine of the faithful at a church service or even a baby asleep in her car seat.

I love you.

The real victims here are the politicians. How can they be expected to do what's morally right when they lost their way, not to mention their souls, so very long ago? These politicians—most of whom have children, grandchildren, maybe even great-grandchildren of their own—have no qualms about walking past grief-stricken parents who clutch photos of their murdered children to their chests and telling them in so many words, "You don't have to go home but you can't cry here."

They have to know, deep down, what they're doing is wrong, and the world certainly knows what they're doing is wrong, but they put their suits on like it's any other job, or maybe they're convinced they're righteous people doing God's work. But they are no more doing God's work than the ones who have pulled the trigger over and over again.

And again.

And yet again.

Ad infinitum.

I love you.

We need to keep our sympathies where they belong—with the powerful and the armed. With those who feel threatened in the face of the most toothless efforts to stem the bloodshed and those who believe scary stories about their guns being taken away. Let's face it; it would be easier to take away the ocean or the stars. Did you know there are more guns than people in this country? That means everyone in your class already has a gun with their name on it, so to speak. Maybe mention that at share time.

I love you.

You could also tell your class that sometimes when I hear a lot of ambulances and fire trucks go by, sirens filling the air with panic, I pay close attention to whether they're heading in the direction of your school. And if they are, I check Twitter and our town hashtag and the fire department account to see if anyone's mentioned your school. When I get the all clear I think, *Someone else's tragedy today, suckers!*

And sometimes I wonder, what if one or both of you gets murdered at school? How will I ever forgive myself for sending you there? You know, to school. But do you want to know what makes me feel better? The fact that you could be massacred pretty much anywhere these days! Such a relief, right? So off you go!

I love you.

Yes I know, I know, you're going to be late. Just to wrap up, our country has chosen to shift all the weight regarding your safety away from our lawmakers and gun manufacturers and instead put it squarely on the shoulders of your principals and teachers. These people who kneel down on the first day of school so they're just as tall as you. These people who shake your hand and say, "Good morning!" and help you rehearse for the school play and take you on field trips to see different rock formations—they are now in charge of keeping you from getting murdered. Which really is the least they can do for all that money they make.

I love you.

Oh hey, quick reminder, tell your teacher I'll be picking you up at two o'clock for your dentist appointment.

And please don't get murdered at school today.

I love you.

I Don't Care If You Go to College

I understand by the simple fact of your birth I was automatically entered in the parental Thunderdome, this arena of demanding you always be in the best-of-the-best-of-the-best possible situations. Where you should learn to nap better than other babies and say the alphabet better than other kindergarteners and take classes that are superior in all ways to the classes that other, lesser / loser children might take.

I understand we now are supposed to be breeding children in a way that will cause them to advance through various schools and camps, sports teams and volunteer opportunities, in a way that shoots them directly through the childhood pipeline and on to Greater Success™. Oh, I know, parents want their children to be happy too. Extremely, *extremely* happy. So much happier than everyone else.

This would all be great except I really don't care if we skip the private preschool, the private elementary school, the private middle school, the prep school, or the sleep-away camp that costs seven thousand dollars for two weeks. Are you serious? I was thirty-five before I spent that much money on a car. You can spend all your time right here during the summer, putting your clean clothes away, riding your bike in circles, and being bored for free.

I don't care if you skip every woo-woo school that replaces math with knitting and English with German. These are the same schools that sent me an informational packet as I desperately tried to find a school for you to attend, and it was like receiving a transmission from outer space. When I tried to walk them through what you had experienced in kindergarten and some of your behaviors and how we were working hard to figure all that stuff out, I was met with a "Well, we do teach a . . . *certain range* of children." What's that? I can't hear you. I think the phrase you're struggling to keep clenched between your ass cheeks is *rich and extraordinarily neurotypical.*

I don't care if you skip the extra-extracurricular activities so you can build up your résumé so you can build up your application so you can build up your essay so you can build up your interview potential so you can have a .05 percent chance of getting into a place that is going to leave us a quarter million dollars in debt so you can graduate and not be able to find a job.

I don't care if we opt out of the greatest parenting-off of all time. When I applied to college—and by "applied to college" I mean exactly one college, a state college—the only way you'd know if someone got in is if they told you right to your face or called you on the phone. And maybe you'd call them back and get a busy signal and I swear, my kingdom for a busy signal right now. I wasn't finding out from someone else's parents that my best friend got into Dartmouth while they shoved that news down everyone else's throats via screens we all held in our hands.

I don't care if you apply to Harvard or Yale or Duke or Columbia or Brown. I don't care if you skip the Ivy League, the Seven Sisters, or any other schools that go by nicknames. Are we not grown-ups at that point?

I don't care if you take the road less traveled. Isn't that what we've been telling kids all along only to then say, as things get real, "Just kidding! DEFINITELY take the road most traveled. Otherwise you'll embarrass me in front of my friends."

I don't care if you go to college. College is no longer a guarantee of anything. It is not a promise you will have a job or a path. The world has changed since I went to college, when a degree was an absolute requirement if you wanted to do capital M More.

I don't care if you buck that system, if you see it for what it is. A potential path but not the *only* path. There are so many paths available to you now. A gap year, if you have money, if we have money. Internships and apprenticeships. Exploration and research. It is worth taking the time to be curious, to honor where your interests lie. Looking back and trying to sift through it all, when you have obligations and commitments, children and a mortgage, is a game that is not fun.

This is what I care about—that you and I resist this pressure together. That you think about the big picture and I try to stay out of it, unless you have questions or want to bounce some ideas off of me. But I will not be calling administrators or program directors or HR on your behalf. I will not be smoothing the way for you, although it will be so hard to resist doing just that. I will have to be the elder grown-up here, to not hobble you with my help. You must find your own way, no matter what way that is.

I am not suggesting you retire to our nonexistent country home to sort this out. This is not an excuse to laze about, to spend your parents' money. First of all, we don't have any money. Second, you can be curious while flipping burgers or pumping gas, fighting wildfires or making coffee. Honest work is good work. It will never fail the core of you. It may not make you rich, but there will be nothing to regret.

I have already been a teenager, a college student, a graduate, a first-job-haver, a quitter, a twenty-year-old, a thirty-year-old, and a failure. I have also been resilient, a winner, and a figured-it-outer. I have already made my own choices and taken my own hits; the time will come for you to make and take yours.

Of course I care what you do with your life. I care very, very much. And if college is ultimately where you want to go and the case can be made for it and it won't bankrupt every last one of us? Then, by all means, have at it. But I will not ask you to determine your life based on mine, your path based on anyone else's, or to set goals based on what my friends' children are up to.

I will be here to listen to you and to guide you, as much as I can or as little as you would like. I will undoubtedly take the wind out of your sails on occasion, but that is the danger of knowing too much. Still, share your cockamamie schemes with me anyway; many a successful career has been launched by just this sort of parental doubting. And I will hang on to the belief that you will be fine. You will be absolutely fine, even if I have to say it over and over again so I don't freak out with worry.

I care about everything you do. But mostly? I care that this is your life. *Yours.*

TIME-OUT

What Do You Think of My Son's Senior Picture That Was Shot by Annie Leibovitz?

Wow, senior year. Hard to believe, isn't it? Seems like just yesterday we were hanging out on the sidelines of the soccer field commiserating over tiny cups of lukewarm apple cider while these guys took shots on the wrong goal, doesn't it? Time flies; time really just flies.

The end of senior year; the end of high school; the end of so much. But to new beginnings, am I right? Cheers to that, I mean, it's been a haul.

Speaking of senior year, did you see Ethan's senior picture? Yes, the one with the tiger. The one shot by Annie Leibovitz? Yes, that's the one. She took a portfolio of images, actually. You really should see the director's cut, or whatever you call it, of that tiger picture. It's wide enough to fill a gatefold in, say, *Vanity Fair's* Hollywood issue. Sure, I guess all their issues are the same size, if you want to be particular about it. I'm just saying I think you've only seen the wallet version, which—while still being mind-blowing, don't get me wrong—really is such a bastardization of Annie's vision. I call her Annie.

I'm not gonna lie, standing around some jungle in Bangladesh watching my firstborn being slowly surrounded by eight Bengal tigers while Annie's twelve assistants and the guy with the tranquilizer gun were frankly a little too far away to really do anything if shit went down for real was a little nerve-racking. But we've raised Ethan to be a creative, freethinking, socially aware, kind-to-animals, risk-taking future astrophysicist and humanitarian triathlete with model good looks, so why stop now? Never quit, unless that's what you'd prefer, that's what I always say.

Look, Jim and I said we wanted something different than that local photographer and his prepackaged over-the-shoulder, tilted-head, soft-focus faux-sunset-and-gazebo poses, and boy did we ever get it. I'm not sure the $4,350 worth of custom-made tiger leis—that weren't even used, PS—were necessary, but who am I to tell Annie Leibovitz that? I'm nobody, that's who. I'm just the person writing the checks. So many checks.

I guess my second favorite picture from *Ethan's Transitions: A Portfolio* by Annie Leibovitz was the one where he's half-submerged in a bathtub filled with pale cherry blossoms and only his bare limbs and unshaven face are poking out. Jim said it felt derivative of her milk-bath Whoopi Goldberg shot but, seriously, Jim? Stick to being a part-time dad. For a change.

I don't think anyone realizes how much attention she puts into every single detail. Even the details that no one, not even those of us on set or paying for said details, would notice in a million years. She hired twenty-two virgins to de-stem every single cherry blossom. You heard me. You know, cherries, de-stemming, virgins, et cetera et cetera. My mind was blown by the way she took such a lowbrow concept of sexuality and transformed it. This was no Warrant's "Cherry Pie," that's for goddamn sure. And, yes, it took six hours for the whole virgins and de-stemming thing and it made us go over budget by $36,335, but I think you'll agree the final image is more than worth it. It's just a treasure. A treasure of unaffordable symbolism. There are no other words for it.

I'm also partial to the gladiator one, shot in Scotland. Which just between you, me, and that surveillance van, why Scotland? Aren't gladiators from Rome? I guess it just goes to show that sometimes you need a true artist to question everything you've been spoon-fed about history. Because what I should be asking is "Why *not* Scotland?" along with "Why is everyone flying first-class?" and "WHY IS MEL GIBSON HERE?" Forty pounds of armor, two hundred and fifty extras, one hundred untrained horses, a severe thunderstorm we had to chase in a caravan of twenty rental cars, three production trucks, a weather van, fifty-five livestock trailers, and a handful of loose male lions later, Annie finally captured the image she had so expertly envisioned. Yes that shot alone resulted in overages of close to a million dollars, but how else would Ethan know we love him?

Anyway, while I have you here, I just wanted to say we've so enjoyed being your neighbors. It's just been such a joy raising our kids together, to see them leap through sprinklers in the front yard when they were little, to watch them grow into the wonderful young men they are, and now to watch as they get ready to head off into the world!

Related to that last part, li'l change of plans. We've come to "unschooling" a bit late in the game so we've decided as a family that Ethan is going to delay his start at Columbia this fall and will instead be spending next year (maybe longer!) wandering around in the woods skinning squirrels and whittling. And I'm going to be rejoining the workforce! And Jim is getting a second job. Also, our house is now on the market. Also, our cars. Also, the boat. Also, my wedding dress. Also, do you know anyone who wants to buy my wedding ring?

But we just couldn't be happier with Ethan's senior pictures, you know? I mean, Annie Leibovitz!

Anne-Marie Slaughter Is My Safe Word

Hey . . . you. Can we talk? Don't worry, it's nothing bad, I just think we should maybe talk a little bit about our relationship. I'm not going to ask you where things are going or anything like that. I mean, that seems a little premature.

Do you remember that game where you add "in bed" to the fortunes in fortune cookies? It's more like that. I want to talk about our relationship . . . in bed. It just seems like we're spending a lot of time together and it feels like things are getting serious. I mean obviously not *serious-serious*. Not marriage serious. What I'm trying to say is we're doing it. A lot. And maybe we're ready to take things to the next level on that front. Feel free to chime in here, but I'm thinking maybe we could do some role-playing, some light bondage, a little spanking or whatever. You know, move things in more of a *Fifty Shades of Grey*–ish direction but with way better writing and worse lighting.

Before you say anything, I'm just here to tell you, yes. YES. Let's go for it. Do you want to go for it? I think we should go for it.

But before we do, we should probably set some ground rules. I don't want to make it seem like I have a ton of experience with this sort of thing, but this one article—okay fine, it was more like six different articles on *Bustle* that I read over and over again— said we should have safe words. So just in case things get a little too rough or out of control we can bring things to a screeching halt before anyone gets hurt.

Are you okay? You look pale.

I know I'm probably catching you a bit flat-footed here, but I've given this a lot of thought. I mean, honestly it's all I think about. Both the rough-sex part and the safe-word part. I've been thinking about my safe word nonstop for the past six months. Yes, I realize we've only been together for like eight weeks or something. I'm allowed to think about things.

Anyway, I want to share my safe word with you. I feel like this is a really big step for me. I mean, for us, you know, as a couple. Ready? Okay. Here goes.

My safe word is *Anne-Marie Slaughter*.

Now I know that's a mouthful, ball-gag puns aside, but I feel like it reflects my beliefs about where we're going as a country when it comes to the intersection of work, parenting, and caregiving in general. Plus I think it's a pretty saucy way of honoring the woman who wrote "Why Women Still Can't Have It All" because if ever there was a gold mine of role-playing inspiration, that piece is it. I know it's not like we have kids or are married or have even been dating—or whatever it is we're doing—for all that long, but I think it's important to always be thinking of the relationship between family-leave policy and rough sex whenever possible. Whether that's with you or whomever I role-play with next.

I know what you're thinking. You're probably thinking, *Seems like* Anne-Marie Slaughter *is a lot to get out in the heat of the moment*, and you're right. So although this is probably against the rules of choosing a safe word, I've taken the liberty of coming up with other options including *lead parent, family leave*, or in a pinch—that reminds me, should we incorporate pinching?—*caregiver*. I'm also open to using *Andy*. That's the name of her husband. Anne-Marie Slaughter's husband. What? Look, it's short, that's all I'm saying.

I also think, while we're sort of on the subject, that we should talk about some role-playing scenarios now so we don't kill the mood trying to sort it out later. One idea I had is you could take our imaginary baby for a walk in the park while I get an imaginary massage and meet my girlfriends for an imaginary glass of wine that will quickly turn into a very real three glasses of wine before I even know what happened. Then I imaginary come home a li'l bit drunk but you are already imaginary asleep because you're so exhausted from taking care of our sweet imaginary daughter for a change. And I start spanking you like you're a big baby, not because you're into that sort of thing but because I need to find some sort of way of venting my boiling frustration at how you so rarely take the lead at home even though we both created this child together and, PS, I'm actually the fucking breadwinner.

So hot, right?

Another game we could play is "I want to murder you when you imply your time is more important than mine." What? It's just a game. You could say something like, "I have to cancel our dinner tonight even though you've already been prepping and cooking basically all day because I ran into some dude I know from college and we're going to go grab a beer or seven." Remember when you did that last week? Just like *Law & Order*, we could pull scenarios from real life and build on them. Our sex life could be all THIS SHIT IS RIPPED FROM THE HEADLINES except the headlines are our life and nothing ever gets resolved in under an hour.

Maybe we could even play that *chunk chunk* sound in between role-playing and getting a glass of water?

Now back to the murder scenario I was talking about. So you'll say that thing I just said about the dinner and the beer and all that, and then what I'll do is place both my hands around your neck like so and I will try to shake you back and forth just to be overly dramatic.

No, this really has nothing to do with the other night. I'm just using it as a jumping-off point. Jeez, don't take it so seriously! Why are you looking at me like that? Is it because I'm somewhat trying to choke you right now? Hello, I'm *role-playing*. I'm demonstrating how something like this might work. This is what role-playing actually is.

Another example could be that time you told my hot friend Jenny—who just made partner at her law firm—that she should've focused on "fulfilling her biological destiny instead, it would've been hella easier" and "Let me know if you need any help with that." Didn't think I'd find out about that, did you? That's because Jenny isn't a disloyal skank, like *some* people I know and role-play with.

So, to review, the role I was playing just now was Girlfriend-Who-Knows-Everything-You-Say-to-My-Friends-When-I'm-Not-Around and yours was The-Only-Level-of-Drunk-That-Makes-That-Behavior-Acceptable-Is-Dead-From-Alcohol-Poisoning.

Why are you yelling "ANDY! ANDY!" Oh right! Safe word. My bad. Obviously a lot of kinks to work out here. Ahhhhhh kinks! Get it?

Do you want to try coming up with your own safe word or maybe some role-playing scenarios? Just freestyling here, right off the top of my head without giving this any forethought whatsoever, but other scenarios could include: A male boss who's coincidentally called Jim just like my first boss and is a sexually harassing pig and I'll play his assistant just like I was Jim's assistant in real life. And this assistant is earning so little money that I'm, I mean she's, in no position to file a complaint with HR. Or you could play the Republican-led Congress and I'll play all the women in this country and you just fuck me up the ass over and over again while shouting out the rights you're taking away from us.

So dirty, so . . . fucked up.

Oh! Another one is I could be a new mom but since I work for a company with fewer than fifty employees I could get fired while I'm on maternity leave and will have no legal recourse whatsoever. You can play the male head of HR who calls me at home and explains it to me as if I'm a child. Mostly in this scenario I just cry.

The more I think about it, HR is a really rich territory to play around with in general.

Where are you going? We could also just get takeout. Let's get takeout!

What do you have against Anne-Marie Slaughter?

BODIES

Who Does That?

I saw it out of the corner of my eye as we approached the newsstand next to our gate. The *Sports Illustrated* swimsuit issue. The cover where the model is pulling her bikini bottoms down so low, you can almost see London *and* France. The cover that made previous covers look like *Amish Vogue*.

When interviewed, the model said her cover was actually not so naughty and it just must be the Year of the Torso. Unless penises go in torsos and babies come out, someone needs a refresher on anatomy.

I had heard about the manufactured controversy and brushed it off before ever seeing the cover. Just another "scandal" in a lifetime of conversations and accusations focused on the female body. But, seeing that cover, my eight-year-old daughter stopped in her tracks, put her hands on her hips, and pointed. She looked up at me, as a combination of incredulity and genuine curiosity flickered across her face, and asked, "Who *does* that?"

When I told my husband about it, we both laughed. That knowing, superior laugh that parents so often have. That laugh of "We know everything; she/he/they know(s) nothing." That "Oh, so cute, she'll learn one day how things really are." We acted as if *she* was the one who was in the wrong, that one day she would understand that this was just how the world worked.

And the way the world works is like this: if you have a female body you will be existing in a body that invites catcalls, "invites" rape, "invites" assault, invites looks, invites admiration, invites ownership by others, invites jealousy, actively shuns attention, is too covered up, too prudish, too fat, too flabby, too thin (which, admittedly, must be a range that only a dog can hear), too wide-hipped, too small-breasted, too veiny in the legs area, too hairy in all the areas, too dark, too athletic, too masculine, too strong, too old, too invisible, too pregnant, too ewwww postpartum, too breastfeed-y, too momish, too *functional.*

Too human.

When my daughter was two or three, I soaked up the utter delight and pride she felt in her body. Fuck cord blood; *this* is what we should be banking. I wanted to save it for her for later. I wanted to save it for both of us.

Her body worked like it should, and that's all a body needed to do. Her belly stuck out because that's what bellies do. Her arms and legs swung back and forth, pumping the swing, reaching for things she needed to reach, running to wherever she needed to run. Because that's what legs and arms and bodies do.

A body was a vehicle, a means to an end. It was a tool, for getting things and going places. It was something she looked out from and thought, "Where can this take me today? Could it ride a bike with training wheels? Could it jump from the edge of the pool and take me under the water? Could it wiggle and giggle, trying to squirm away from Dad when he tries to tickle me? Could it hop and jump and sleep and eat and move me through this world?"

There is a sadness, a feeling of dread really, that most mothers feel in knowing that this self-assurance and trust our young daughters feel in their bodies is ultimately fleeting. That soon enough they will start to look at their bodies as others do, as something to judge. As something to punish. As something that is no longer theirs. As something separate from themselves. And as something that belongs to the world in a way their brothers' bodies never will.

———

I am seven. I want to be a fashion designer. I drape myself in my grandmother's blankets and fabrics. My friends and I pin a sheet onto her clothesline, using it as a stage curtain, and we put on fashion shows in her backyard. Bodies are beautiful and fun. They're where clothes go.

Bodies take you to the beach down the street and take you into the salt water, wearing beat-up sneakers so the crabs don't pinch your callused feet. Those tough feet have spent all summer naked, hot stepping it down sizzling asphalt and baking sand, scrambling over rocks and broken shells. Bodies that wade into the water and feel seaweed brush past, like a school of green ribbonfish. Bodies that absorb sun and are dead tired by the end of the day. Bodies in motion, bodies at rest.

———

I am ten. I scramble up the hill in my backyard, digging for arrowheads with my bare hands. I sit on a moss-covered rock that I call the Whale, its big flat head and horizontal crack of a mouth carrying me through an ocean of pine needles and foxes, blue jays and dark woods. I flip rotten logs over to find salamanders and pick pebble-size wild blueberries from scrubby bushes. I swing on our rope swing in the front yard, my feet flying over the tops of trees, my hair brushing the ground I'm leaning so far back. I lie on our hammock, sun flickering on my face as I pass underneath the leaves. One of our cats snoozes on my flat, smooth tummy.

I am a child in this world. My body is an antenna, tuning everything in.

———

I am fourteen. I'm very thin, so thin I can still wear clothes from the kids' section.

I have a flat bum and flat chest and haven't gotten my period yet. I'm a late bloomer—that much is obvious.

A boy in my class remarks, "Whatever there is of Kim Harrington you'd have to eat out." Not only do I still not know what the fuck that's supposed to mean, I feel fairly confident that he didn't know what it meant either.

I just knew it was Not Good.

———

I am nineteen and home from college. I have gained at least thirty, if not forty, pounds. I have frosted and permed and bleached the absolute bejesus out of my hair in some sort of desperate attempt to distract from this.

I am driving to a soccer game in my hometown and as I drive by, a few boys turn their heads. They see my blond hair. I have potential. I get out of the car and slam the door behind me.

As I walk, I overhear one of the boys say to the other, "Told you she'd be fat."

I pray I get cancer so I will be reduced to the weight of a skeleton. *Cancer.*

———

I am twenty. I am twenty-five. I am thirty. I can count on one hand the number of times I am happy with my body in those ten years. My weight has gone down, but it doesn't matter, there is always something to not like.

My body is still an antenna, but now it's tuning out. Distorted.

I am thirty-five. And thirty-seven. I had expected the worst from pregnancy. For it to blow apart and ruin my body in ways even my freshman year of college couldn't accomplish. To gain one hundred pounds and never lose it.

Instead, both times that I'm pregnant, I'm in love with the way my body is taking shape. I have the pure thrill of walking into a room, belly first. Realizing for the first time in decades that I'm not trying to suck my stomach in. Because not only would it be impossible, I wouldn't want to if I could. My belly is hard and round and a laser beam focus for smiles. This is what it must feel like to actually like your body. To always have liked your body.

I have regained a childlike sense of at-home-ness in my body. With a miscarriage before my first child and a miscarriage between my first and second, these pregnancies are holding on. I am rooting for my body. You can do it, body!

These pregnancies will result in whole, healthy children. My body did that.

My skin is clear and creamy, my hair the thickest it's ever been. My breasts are as full and firm as they will ever be, for the rest of my life. My belly—my enormous belly—makes the rest of me look small.

I am still breastfeeding my second child, my daughter. She was a big baby when she was born—eleven pounds, nine ounces— and ravenous. I gained sixty pounds during my pregnancy, my waist measuring forty-seven inches a week before she was born. Two weeks later, my waist measures thirty-three inches.

I had bought a pile of Levi's in ever-increasing sizes to wear during my pregnancy; I now make quick work of them on the way back down. My arms are defined from carrying this chunk of a baby as well as hauling around her brother, now two years old and only recently starting to walk. My body is getting taken to the cleaners, no doubt, but it's strong and has purpose. It's no longer about me.

It's a relief for it to no longer be about me.

For the first time since I was prepubescent I need to wear a belt to keep my smallest jeans from falling off my body. I decide this is how models must feel all the time.

It's glorious.

I am forty-seven. My body is changing. It feels like my life was one long chug up a roller coaster to having children. To avoiding pregnancy like the plague, then pursuing it with not-so-quiet desperation. To navigating those pregnancies and post-pregnancies like a cork in a storm. To recovering from it all. For years.

Soon, in the next few years, in the next decade anyway, my period will stop. I have a hard time accepting this. It feels like the end of possibility.

My body is an antenna, and it's trying to tune in to those faraway stations. The ones that only sound like fuzz. The ones that will tell me what is coming, what to expect. I don't yet understand the language.

I decided to finally answer my daughter's question. Although I couldn't answer it to her satisfaction nor mine. Sure, the model "did" that. But so did the photographer. And the crew. And the retoucher. And the magazine. The subscribers and the buyers. The advertisers and the newsstands. The culture. The men. The world.

"Who does that," I said, "is a really good question. It's more than just the woman you see on the cover."

She just gave me a weird look.

When she was nine, she pointed out the girls in bikinis on the beach. She said, "I don't understand why girls' bottoms stick out of their bathing suits but boys' butts don't. That's not fair."

I thought, *That's just how the world works.* Again. But instead I caught myself and said, "You're right. It *isn't* fair."

She is not a child who is modest. She spends almost all her time in our house in nothing but underpants, even in the winter. But she understands public versus private. And in public, she wants her body covered. It's her body, hers. And she wants to determine who will see the curve of her bottom where it meets her legs. *She* decides.

She asked if I would get her board shorts next summer.

I said what I should've said all along, what I need to keep saying, to her, to myself, with pride, "Of course. It's *your* body."

If You Can Touch It

"He's pretty enough to be a girl."

That's what a nurse said when you were one day old. And unlike my don't-call-my-daughter-beautiful-call-her-smart and don't-call-my-son-smart-call-him-kind Vermont neighbors, I took this compliment to heart. I knew what she meant. I was on her side.

In the almond-shaped eye of the storm, I held you. You with your bent ear from being stuffed up against my rib cage, facing the wrong direction, but closer to my soft, wild heart. A position you continue to hold as you grow older, ear now unfolded, and yet sometimes you're still facing the wrong way, according to other people anyway. But you are always, always closer to the core of me.

Your foot also bent, we thought a consequence of your odd position too, only to discover later—through my newfound motherly suspicion and not the young pediatrician who kept telling us it would work itself out—this is *not* going away. Something is wrong. I knew this.

If only I always had that insight, that confidence, to throw off the world around us.

If only I could always know there's a fix for whatever might hobble you.

If only.

I held you in the hospital over those first few days, the days when you didn't know how to nurse and I didn't know how to nurse you and I had a postpartum exhaustion breakdown. "How could I be failing *already?*" and then, realizing it was Father's Day, I looked up through my tear-stained face and said, "Happy first Father's Day" to your dad in the most "What a fucking shit show this is already, huh?" tone of voice I could muster.

Even during those days, as I watched you sleep, your chest and belly alternating with deep, puffy baby breaths like a seesaw built on clouds, I thought, *How could anyone ever get mad at their kid?*

It didn't take long before I could answer, "Quite easily actually."

We are alike, you and I. Sometimes it's like fighting with a mirror. We blow up and swirl away from each other, sometimes screeching and other times a sweeping cold front of silent anger and frustration. When you are seething with anger and don't want anyone to even think of touching you, boy do I know how you feel.

But you are still the age when you want me to sit with you at night, before you fall asleep, to talk about everything except what we were fighting about. You still want me near, though I feel you pulling your own way. And I want to be near, to you, always.

I tell you, "There is nothing you can do that would make me not love you. I don't care how angry we get at each other. I will always love you. You know that, don't you?"

I say it, often, because when you're angry you accuse me of not loving you—worse, of not even caring about you at all—of loving your sister more, your perfect sister. I know how deep that hurt must go for you to spit those words at me when you're at your most open.

I'm not sure there is a worse accusation, to not even care,

when I have turned myself inside out for you. Have I done enough? No mother in history ever has.

But an accusation like this at age eleven is very different than a stomping accusation at age four. At four there is time. At four, it's cute. Now I feel the whoosh of time, of time wanting to take you away from me. And will you be ready? Will I be ready? Have I done right by you?

I now understand the phrase *leaps and bounds*. It started two years ago, you wanting to jump and tap every doorjamb with your fingertips. Everything just above your head, and just out of reach. Run, jump, stretch, tap! Or miss. So close.

You are measuring yourself against the world. You know you take up more space, but you still feel small. You stretch out in your bed and say, "Look how long I am!" and I say, "It's easy to see that in this bed, you've had this bed since you were maybe three or four!" It's a measuring stick you sleep on, how your feet have grown closer to the footboard and now you can easily touch both the headboard and footboard at the same time, without even trying.

And then you say, "But when I'm at school, I don't feel as long."

"As tall, you mean."

"As tall."

I tell you that's because you're in a bigger world there. There are grown-ups to compare yourself to and that's not a fair comparison. But in your class? You're one of the tallest.

"That's because I'm older."

"Partly, yes."

We held you back—I held you back; I made that decision. To keep you from going to first grade, to stop the runaway train that had you cowering under tables in kindergarten, afraid of everything, loud sounds and toilets, impending fire drills and rowdy boys who slashed and burned.

We homeschooled you for a year or, as I like to say, "home-schooled" you, quote unquote. What we really did was spend a year trying to figure you out, away from school days that ground us down. You went to OT and PT, to a social-thinking group and a therapist. You started piano lessons that year because I wanted you to have some kind of fun. But to you, most of it was fun. Five years later you still talk about the pool at PT and the little cars you got to ride on and the games you were able to play. You say you miss it.

That makes one of us.

This year you've made a point of telling me you would already be in middle school now, if we hadn't held you back, if not for *that* year. It's one of the very few times I tell you I regret nothing. That it was the right decision and you will never convince me otherwise. That you needed that time, we needed that time, and what we did then has made all the difference now.

You can't imagine how rare that sort of certainty is.

You have come so far. And we will never know what pushed you forward. Was it all of those early interventions or was it holding you back or was it simply the fact that you are you and you matured and found your own way? It doesn't matter to me. There are no awards ceremonies at the end of this. I just know you are doing so well, even if you don't see it. Maybe that's why when things blow up, it feels so much worse than it used to. And that's really saying something, because it used to feel plenty awful.

I understand now how spectacularly a person can fuck up when they've relied on physical presence, on height, to impose discipline. You're to my cheek now and soon you will be taller than me. Who will be towering over whom then? Pointing fingers and yelling?

As we continue to slowly separate from each other, I hope

somewhere in your bones you'll remember that almond-shaped eye of the storm where we began. Your bent ear. My stomach lashed closed and bandaged. A bruised-and-battered team.

You would fall asleep in my arms. Mine was the lightest sleep. I slept on couches with my back bent, woke to hear your quiet breathing. Happy. Needed.

From those mornings on, I have always wondered what is going on inside of your brilliant, complicated mind. I will always wonder. That mind that can figure out a song by ear and bring me to tears when I hear it from two rooms away. That mind that can break and remake things, because you can see it, right there, how to create, without instructions. That mind that thinks everyone in your class hates you, that we don't love you, that the world is against you, that other adults—strangers—are the only people you can trust and the only ones who get you.

In an age of bullying—and you have been bullied—there is one thing now that drives me crazier than all of it. That when you point out the window, thrilled, to see a fire truck or a police car, that the kids in your class will fake exclaim, "Oooooh WOW, that's so cool," and then let their eyes go dead to show you how uncool it actually is.

I hate those kids. Politically correct everything aside, I want to punch those kids hard, right in the sternum, knock the breath right out of them. Those little fuckers. The ones who step on your heart, using it as a rung to inch their way up the most pathetic of social ladders. The ones who give your sometimes socially imprecise mind false hope that you've found a kindred spirit only to confirm, uh *no*, you definitely have not. Eye roll.

I tell you to not let them kill that part of you that fills up with excitement and wonder; it's what will carry you further than they will ever go. That your curiosity and sensitivity is a gift. That being cool is incredibly overrated. That those kids may be as cool as they ever get and look how they're using it. By being a bunch of dicks.

Keep being excited, I practically command. Don't let the bastards get you down.

Those kids are probably the same kids who watch you out of the side of their faces when you wave to me from the school bus. You are in fifth grade and you still wave to me as I stand in our living room window with a coffee in my hand. I see your round face in the window, waving and watching me wave back until we lose sight of each other. Every once in a while I catch myself tearing up and I think, *I will always remember you like this. I will always think of these mornings, you waving to me from the school bus, the most open face, full of love, never shifting your gaze until I disappear from your sight.*

It feels like a thumb being pressed on my heart in those moments, as if to throw off the weight of a scale. It feels heavier than it should.

Maybe it's because in those little slivers, I think, *You know that I get you. Not always, but we will always have an understanding, you and I. We're not always easy people, but we are worth it. I think so anyway.*

The first time I saw you struggle, really struggle, maybe you were four. You would blow up and be defiant or implode over some of the navigations and nuances we all take for granted.

I thought:

Make it through middle school, make it through high school.

You will find your people.

You will have a great life.

You have one now, I think, but it really will get better.

So when you started saying you wish you were dead, that maybe you shouldn't be here, you were maybe seven or eight.

And it sounded like you meant it, that you understood the words you were saying.

I suddenly burst into tears and held your arms, maybe too tightly, and said, "Please promise me you will never hurt yourself. *PROMISE ME.*"

We were both surprised by how seriously I took your words; I think we were both scared. I know we were.

Promise me you will never leave me, is what every mother, every parent is saying, even if they don't realize it. We are all saying it from that very first breath.

Don't you dare take yourself away from me, when the world is so full of forces that are more than happy to do it for you. Don't you dare make that happen, so help me God.

Don't you dare put that thought out into the world, because now it's in my head and it's in yours. And the very worst part—the universe has heard it too.

It's there.

Lurking and marinating.

Just add anger or humiliation or sadness and it froths up to the surface again.

Don't you dare do this to me.

To you.

To us.

Don't you dare.

The morning of my birthday, as I drove from coffee to errands to home, I heard a poem on the radio that knocked me out, for reasons I couldn't quite put my finger on. Then again, that's poetry isn't it?

This being Vermont, we ended up living right down the street from that poet, Julie Cadwallader Staub, two years later. I soon put together the puzzle that one of her twin daughters worked in my kids' first elementary school and the other one managed the farm we obsessively visited.

I finally met her when she joined us for a neighborhood Green Up Day, my kids having designed and papered our neighborhood with an invitation to pick up trash. After a few minutes of stomping through the little creek down the hill, dodging pricker bushes and throwing old bottles and broken plastic flowerpots into trash bags, I told her how much I loved her poem, the one I had heard on *The Writer's Almanac*. Like any accomplished and not-easily-flattered Vermonter she said, "Which one? There are quite a few."

We don't wear makeup; we wear mud boots. This is a good place to raise kids, to be a writer, to spend the first warm sunny Saturday picking up trash after an unforgiving winter.

Before the poem, before this neighborhood, as her daughters became familiar faces in my kids' lives I thought, *Those girls (women!) are such wonderful people. Their parents must be so proud of them. Whatever they did, I want to do.*

I still do. I'm trying.

Oh that feeling
of running as fast as I could
extending my arms, my hands, my fingers
as far as I could
watching that spiraling bullet of a football,
reminding myself:
if you can touch it,
you can catch it.

If you can touch it,
you can catch it.

You still leap to slap your fingertips against the doorjamb, to brush the fringe of the basketball net, to shove a long stick into the tree to get a Frisbee, a football, another stick, a ball, a parachuting GI Joe down from our half-dead tree.

One day you will simply reach up and touch those things, it will be easy because they will just be there. Easily within your grasp. Because you will be longer and you will be taller.

Until then I watch you leap and stretch, hand flat, fingers wiggling:

If you can touch the frame of your future life, even a little bit, you will reach it.

If you can feel the feathery edges of your potential and your promise, even in the most abstract way, you will get there.

If you imagine yourself away from us, woven in with the people who fit you, the other family we all assemble away from our parents and siblings, from the way we grew up, you will more than survive. You will thrive.

I repeat it like a prayer.

If you can touch it, you can catch it.

If you can touch it, you can catch it.

Amen.

As Young as We'll Ever Be

Every summer we spend time in Maine. The same beach my grandparents brought my dad and his brothers to. The same one my dad brought me to. The same one my kids now race each other to.

I remember being eight years old, splashing through the glassy waves with my unruly girl feet. An olive drab nylon backpack bouncing against my back, nothing inside to weigh it down except for a single plastic collapsible drinking cup. I don't remember drinking from that cup, but I remember its design. When expanded, each circle step building on the other, holding water. And when it was collapsed down flat, it had the feel of a giant checker. How could anything like that even remotely work?

I've returned to this beach over and over again, as a teenager and as a college student. I brought my best friend from high school, then another from college, then my boyfriend, who became my husband. Passing acquaintances were not allowed. People who might feel snobbish about camping, squeamish about mosquitoes, or expect modern conveniences in a fancy setting could keep moving. I required commitment. I required people who were open to loving this place as much as I always had.

There is an understanding here. There are no radios blaring wah-wah car dealership commercials. Most people bring horseshoes, a football, or books instead. This beach is for relaxing and reflecting. It's for connection. It is not an amusement park. It is not a club.

The one mirror in our cottage (it's a rental, but it's ours) is ancient and clouded, hung at a level that only allows adults to see themselves from the clavicle up. I don't wear makeup or bother with a cover-up for my swimsuit-clad middle-aged body as I walk from the cottage to the beach and back to use the bathroom, get a drink, or grab a fresh towel. There is no one here to impress. It's the closest I ever come to inhabiting my body like a small child, trusting and admiring its function.

We are laid bare here. This is not the beach of the beautiful people. It's the beach for the rest of us.

A year passes.

Kids tumble down to the beach on the first day and my breath catches at how much they've grown. A little boy who was pushing a dump truck on the beach last summer is recognized solely by the dump truck. He's taller, more sure-footed. Without the same toy, it would've taken longer for my brain to match the former to the present.

A freckle-faced nine-year-old girl from last summer now looks that much closer to the freckle-faced teenager she will soon be. And new babies arrive. Teenagers return and bring a friend with them. College kids come and everyone's coupled up. Married couples walk their dogs and parents relish the freedom to let their kids run, yell, and sing as loudly as they want. No one can outshout the waves.

There are the girls in their early teens, with the gangly limbs of children and the growing bodies of women. They romp in the waves not fully realizing the complicated power their bodies possess. They absentmindedly grab their budding breasts to adjust their tops, and I put my head in my hands. They don't even know. Or maybe they do.

One summer a mother and her two teenage girls lounged on a blanket next to us. They were very Vermont—the mother with long and wild gray hair and a cloth tote bag full of books, the girls slim and athletic with chestnut hair tangling in the wind. The older girl played board games and cards with her mother when the wind was still. The younger daughter, who was maybe fourteen and wore a simple bikini, lay on her side, directly on the hot sand. She sifted sand between her fingers for almost an hour letting it fall, her long hair lifting and falling to the side with the breeze. At ease.

I was shocked to feel tears spring to my eyes as I watched her. *I will never be that age again,* I thought. *I will never have a body like that, ever. I will never again feel like I have my whole life ahead of me. I can only go forward from here, if I'm lucky.* I reached for my beach towel and shoved it under my sunglasses.

There are middle-aged mothers in skirted bathing suits, shoulders hunched from the weight of raising children. There are middle-aged fathers bodysurfing with their kids, energized by the absence of work, restored to their young selves with the blind optimism of what their bodies can do. Finding out the hard way that maybe they actually can't anymore. Sunburns and pulled muscles. Nothing a few beers can't take care of.

There is a man in his fifties who sits in a webbed folding chair, the nylon kind with an aluminum frame that you always used to see at barbecues and backyard parties. Every day he has a bottle of water tucked under one elbow as his other arm involuntarily flaps at his side. Parkinson's, most likely. Each knee marked with a long vertical scar, double plus signs from a distance. The zinc sunscreen under each eye, suddenly the marks of a warrior.

There is a group of ladies in their sixties, gathered under their umbrellas since breakfast. They drink Bloody Marys every morning, at least two of them holding a cup or wearing a T-shirt with the telltale pink ribbon.

There is the elderly woman whose legs are as big as tree trunks, swollen and red with skin drawn taut. Her husband anticipates her every move and need, holds her loose bandages that trail in the wind behind her like streamers, her walking becoming more difficult with each passing year. The perimeter of her travels has grown ever smaller, from the beach one year to the viewing deck the next and now to just standing on the walkway, and only for a few minutes at a time, just to look out at the raging ocean and feel the breeze on her face. So much power, so little power.

Simple ability and movement suddenly feel like fierce gifts instead of givens. I think of how easily I walk into the waves or navigate the hot sand path to the beach. How I unthinkingly go through the motions of assisting children or lugging things back to the cottage without help, a packhorse. I think about loyalty and love, vows and vulnerability.

We can never know what's coming. We can't know what's heading our way a year from now; we can't know it just for tomorrow. I look around and think constantly, *We are all fragile; we are all strong.*

I look back at photos of me when my son was a year old. I remember that at the time I thought I looked awful, old. I look at those pictures now and think of how young I look. My skin looks smooth. I know I'm tired, but I look happy. I was happy.

I look in the mirror now and trace the deep crease between my eyebrows, the one that etched itself from forty-seven years of not believing what I was seeing. My neck is getting looser, the skin on my chest telling all kinds of truths. The sun has done its damage. So has time.

But five and ten and twenty years from now, I will look at

pictures of me that were taken last week and think of how young I look. What was I complaining about? I must've been tired. But I looked happy. I was. I am.

This is all of us, every year. We fill up. We collapse. Over and over again. But for now, we are here. As young as we'll ever be.

Hot-Ass Chicks

When I am looking for you, I see you.

You are walking briskly on your lunch break with your co-worker, both in sensible sneakers and office-appropriate attire. Not power attire, more like a top and slacks. That word *slacks* just says it all, doesn't it? You absentmindedly tug at your top, it's a habit now. Trying to create space between the fabric and your blubby tummy or goddamn hips. Your words.

Back at your desk you probably brought your own lunch and a healthy afternoon snack. That vending machine is the biggest slut in the office, always ready to put out for anyone with small bills and an appetite. You are forever on the defense.

I see you see yourself. You catch your reflection in a passing mirror or the dentist office's window or on your phone because the camera was accidentally set on reverse and is there anything worse in the entire universe than *that*? You think no one is watching—because no one ever is—so you smooth your hair, you press your fingertips between your eyebrows wishing it was a hot iron, pressing out the divot that has slowly carved its way into your flesh, the divot that broadcasted your doubt when you were twenty-five. Now you are permanently doubtful. You gently pull at the far corners of your eyes, or maybe under your jawline, and you can still see the smoother, sharper you. She's in there. It feels as though she was just there a little while ago. If you could just make these tugs permanent, these little adjustments. You stop what you're doing. It just makes you sad.

I see you from behind, and you have the bottom of a twenty-something but when I pass you on the sidewalk I have the same reaction men must have—yikes, you're like fifty! Your body is the opposite of so many of those other middle-aged bodies but somehow I still sense your inner monologue and its relentlessness, your inability to let yourself off the hook, your unwillingness to accept this is the stage of life you're in now. I sense your fear. Your fear you are disappearing, that those eyes you grew accustomed to lingering upon you simply because you existed, those eyes are elsewhere now. Your fear that if heads aren't turning, then what's the point, really? Am I wrong? Your Bikram and CrossFit, tanning and raw foods; your no sugar, no alcohol, no bread, no pasta, no fats, no dessert, and all what-the-fuck-is-this-shit diet. You made a deal with the devil in exchange for a great-looking ass. You adhere to a complex Jenga of rules that barely make sense for models and actresses, all in an attempt to get back what you didn't used to have to work for. You were just . . . you. Firm and beautiful, young and resilient, clueless and wanted. Who needed a personality back then?

I'm guessing it never occurred to you when you looked down on older women, the ones you assumed weren't even making an effort, one day you'd discover all the effort in the world still won't make you sixteen, twenty-two, thirty again. Sometimes all the effort in the world can't even make you a marginally better forty-eight.

Oh I know, honey. You do it to feel good. You do it for mental-health reasons and just to feel more confident. Me too. It has nothing to do with my pants or thighs or post-childbirth tummy or my bat wings or my neck or my age or my life or my struggle against mortality. Obviously! I'm sure if magazine covers,

Instagram, and every corner of our cultural press paid the most slaving attention to nothing but forty-five-year-old women who hovered right around a size 14, we'd still be doing all of this stuff, right?

Of course we would. Wouldn't we?

What about your face? You can't exercise that. Ugh the face, it always gives it away, doesn't it? But if you monkey with your face, well, you best be prepared to apologize to the world for being so vain.

Now, why on earth would you be so vain?

It's a mystery wrapped in a just-go-die-already fortune cookie, isn't it?

I say I see you. But I only see you when I'm looking for you. Because no one really sees middle-aged women, do they? They don't see we are the same girls we were before. That our laughs are the same and the way our hair always curled in that one particular spot, that's the same too. That our stories are the same as they were before, as are the jokes; they just come out of a mouth that is softer. The lip line less crisp.

I see you, and I will think how middle-aged you look. How you are obviously older than I am. Then somehow I will find out you are actually younger. By a lot. And I will realize I'm comparing your outside to my inside, because my inside is a solid twenty-eight or thirty-two max. And I will see me, finally. I will catch the reflection of my fleshy triceps-ish area in the mirror. What the fuck! That's certainly not my arm, not the way it rolls over like that, with not a small amount of momentum. That's the arm of a neighbor lady in Rhode Island, arms poking out of a shapeless shift, a housedress, a Tab in one hand and Newports in the other. It has to be. That splotchy ham hock can't be mine.

And I see the spots from those early years of lying around beaches listening to shitty music, absent of sunscreen and present of baby oil and Sun In. I see the skin on my forearm, crinkling like birthday streamers in response to the slightest pressure. That's the skin of my mother and my grandmother before her. That's the skin I clearly never planned on having. But there it is, right on my own arms. Well, this is certainly ridiculous.

I see the fading fox tattoo on the inside of my wrist, the one I got when I was twenty because I thought it would protect me from ever having a corporate job. Obviously no one would give a serious job to a person with a single tattoo the size of a quarter. So adorable.

I should feel grateful for living this long, for being healthy, for being here at all. My kids' classmates have lost parents, a mother to suicide, a mother to cancer, another mother to cancer. When I hear this news, I am crushed, even though these were not my friends. Because as he curls into bed my son will tell me, "We were waiting for you guys to show up at the concert and I asked my friend where his mom was and he said she died in January," and like in a movie, my hand automatically claps over my heart and I gasp.

"Oh my God, that's awful."

I feel the mundane and utter blandness of my normal-ass days and all my complaining about pants smash against a rock. I think about this alternate reality where I don't miss your school concerts because I am out of town or have a meeting but because I am dead. And I will never see another anything that you're in. I will never see anything about you again. You will know it every day, that I can't be there like the other mothers because I will never be anywhere. I go to bed that night, I drive to the bank the next day, I take the dog for a walk, and for weeks afterward I whisper to myself, "Please, please, please don't let anything happen to me."

So, yes, in the words of my friend Kate's father: "It beats the alternative." Aging beats being dead.

That is my positive review of aging.

But I'll tell you what, when I look at my friends, I see them. I really see them. And truth be told, they are some hot-ass chicks. I'm jealous of their good bums and strong arms; the thick hair, open ears, and utter can-do-ness they possess. They are brave, not in the same exact ways, which is crucial. I see them whole, and if I notice a softening jawline or a dimple anywhere but on their cheeks, those are just features and those are just facts. Like whether the sun is rising or if there's a storm blowing in. Those are not the entirety of who these grand women are. They're not even a decent percentage.

That jawline is not their laugh, and those dimples are not the tears we've let loose at birthday dinners or midweek cocktails, coffee dates or Christmas parties. The tears from laughter and frustration, from fear, from the subset of sadness that comes when you tell people who you really are and hope against hope they won't turn away.

It's one thing to have acquaintances at this age. It's quite another to be able to say the worst things, the saddest things, the most complain-y things—which you, through habit, will quickly follow up with, "I'm sorry, I'm bringing everyone down." And just as quickly the responses will fly back, "Shut up, this is what this is all about. This is what we're supposed to be about."

We are trained to compliment-sandwich our way through life. Our lives, our husband's lives, the lives of our children, our employers, our employees, every figure of authority, and every peer. We must facilitate everyone's fragility and be more than happy to do it. We especially must do this with other women because are we not all on the same side?

I'm here to tell you: we are not.

Nothing will make that more clear than a presidential election or being the mother of school-aged children. I have continuously been dragged and dropped into peer groups I would rather lick doorknobs than be a part of. It's a maze of ugh, from school to sports, plays to birthday parties. Who the fuck are these people? The only thing we have in common is that we bred. And yet I guess that's an invitation for this one over here to tell me her opinion on public versus private education even though she knows through the grapevine I'm currently homeschooling out of straight-up desperation and struggling to find the best fit, any fit that works, regardless of the philosophies of PEOPLE I DIDN'T ASK. Or I guess the fact that we're standing here on this sideline is like a siren call this other one can't quite resist, assuming our forced physical proximity and Saturday-morning captivity provide just enough things in common to force the most excruciating conversation this side of a Mormon cocktail party. Why do theoretical adults care about high school mascots? Who gives a fuck what choices this coach or that PTO president makes? Why are we discussing screen time? We're outside. Why are you letting your entire life be defined by your kids? Remember hobbies? You should get some. Remember silence? Let's enjoy some together.

Not surprisingly, I am not a good representative for how ladies are supposed to act. We are supposed to go along to get along. Cluck like hens in the henhouse, always something to cluck-cluck about. Doesn't matter if anyone's listening, doesn't matter if there's really anything to say, doesn't matter if you don't even like the person you're talking to and they don't particularly care for you either. It's such a massive waste of everyone's time. And ladies don't have time to waste.

Sometimes you can feel the judgments happening in real time, when even a hint of vulnerability or honesty can send the

inner scorekeepers scrambling up to the scoreboard to update
the numbers. I think back to moments when I've jumped into
conversations (always with the thought, *Look at me! I'm turning
over a new leaf!*), assuming the kind of quick and funny chat I'd
have with my real friends. And before I even know what's happening, I'm suddenly sharing worries and revealing doubts in a
school hallway or on the playground. Even though I know—I
know—I should stop talking, I keep trying to bury my openness
with more openness. It's like my own mouth is swallowing me
whole. It dawns on me, way too late, that I've mistaken opera-
tives for opportunities and now I can't stuff my words back in my
mouth fast enough. I am talking to the absolutely wrong people.
And oof, am I crying now?! Am I getting goddamn emotional?
Bloody hell. One of them will stand stock-still in front of me as
I carry on, with just the slightest, almost imperceptible, grin or
raised eyebrow of satisfaction that says in this one realm at least,
she has her shit together.

Not surprisingly, I've walked away from these interactions
angry at myself for being vulnerable and for assuming ye olde
sisterhood contract with women I'm not even remotely friends
with. What the fuck? I'll feel blue for the rest of the day.

The other day my daughter asked me, "Do you ever have
a feeling like you're sad and you don't know about what? You'll
just be by yourself thinking, and then it's just there. Or you'll
remember something that happened and think, *Oh*, and get sad
all over again." And I was like, "Girl, welcome to being a girl."
Sometimes there are so many things to feel unspecifically and
very specifically sad about.

That's why I need these hot-ass chicks like I need oxygen.
Because the first casualty of motherhood is honesty. And the second is vulnerability. The third is a sense of humor. Wait, that
might be first.

I need these hot-ass chicks because they do not play this "Everything is great, everything is fine, you can't see how hard and fast my feet are paddling under the water over here, right?" game that we learned to play simply by being born female.

We all know no one wants to hear girls complain, honey. Now run along.

When we talk, we talk for real. We talk for keeps. And, sure, there is not a small amount of bitching. But then again there is not a small amount of things to bitch about. Sometimes it's frivolous, most of the time it's silly, and all of it is necessary. We have come close to getting thrown out of some very fine establishments; we roll in like some sort of fur-coat-wearing freak show and we do not give a shit. We have worked hard for these moments of utter ridiculousness and over-the-top fanciness, we will group-text the next morning something around thirty-seven times while wearing sweatpants and last night's false eyelashes. We are continuously Cinderella after the ball, except we are the princes we've been searching for.

Sometimes we take turns competing in the Misery Olympics, some of us medaling more often than seems fair. There is caregiving for the generation above and the generation below. There is therapy for our kids and our marriages and ourselves. There are those moments where everything falls apart, all at once. We listen. We know. We can't believe it's this hard. No one told us it'd be this hard.

When we talk, we talk about how we still get fucked with, even now, even after all this time. We are awash in liberal men who think they're just one Women's March away from sprouting a pussy, so of course they can still talk over us and steamroll forward with their plans and then send passive-aggressive e-mails afterward that no matter how many ways you turn them, still don't include the apologies they should. Hot tip: "I'm sorry you feel that way" is not an actual apology, dipshits. We are awash in needing to train husbands to pitch in like it isn't pretty fucking obvious we need help. JUST LOOK AT US. And we are awash in feeling bad about saying anything. Because you're not supposed to say anything; people are just supposed to know. Men are just supposed to know.

(They do not know.)

I need these hot-ass chicks because sometimes what we have in common is what girls have in common, and sometimes what girls have in common is pretty fucked up indeed. We will talk on a hot August night on what was supposed to be a fancy excuse for a midweek night out, and before you know it we're talking about rape and verbal abuse and all the times we thought we might be kidnapped. You know, girl talk.

There was that time when I was ten and my friend and I were walking back from the store near the beach. An old man driving a boat of a car crept along that road, once down and once back. Noticeably slowly. I mean, you have to drive pretty slow in a shitty old car to catch the attention of a couple of chattering ten-year-old girls.

Even as I recall this, my factory-installed gut-reaction-denier kicks in and I think, "Maybe he lost his dog; maybe he was looking for his dog" and Jesus Christ did I not just tell my own ten-year-old daughter two nights ago that she is never to approach nor go with an adult who says they have lost their dog and need the help of a child?

All I know is that on that day, on that hot summer day, most likely walking barefoot and holding on to tiny paper bags full of Swedish fish, licorice ropes, and Smarties, on the third time that car passed us, we took off running. No more waiting around to see what happened next. We sprinted, darted right, and slid down a scrubby embankment, flattening ourselves to the ground like cats. Ears back, tails twitching.

I still remember that golden brown sedan, slowing down where we had last appeared. And that old man searched; I can still see his potato sack of a face looking in the direction of those bushes and grass where we lay still, hearts pounding. Him and his car, his rolling creeper metal suit that glimmered in the hot afternoon sun, it moved along that one block slower than if he had been in a parade.

He hadn't lost a dog. He had lost his chance.

That's what us hot-ass chicks talk about, all those times we got away. And the times we didn't. We will talk about that feeling in our gut that something isn't quite right. We will talk about cowering or running, hiding or slapping. We will talk about how we pass these lessons on to our daughters. Because your options are to give them the tools they need or give them nightmares. Unfortunately, they usually get both.

We will teach them that you need to listen to your gut, don't worry about hurting anyone's feelings, just get out of there. That worrying about hurting a stranger's feelings can be the difference between being alive or being dead.

And we will teach them that if you are lost and afraid, look for a mother with children because she is automatically more trustworthy than any adult man and especially any adult man who is by himself. That you have as much of a right to feel safe and whole as anyone else, that you don't owe anyone anything, that being nice is so fucking overrated and you might as well learn that now. Nice can be a trap your entire life.

That is only the beginning of the lessons we teach. Not because those lessons are part of a radical feminist agenda, but because our daughters need to know these things as much as they need to learn *please* and *thank you*, where babies come from, and how to use a tampon. Because this is what it's like to be a girl and a woman in this country, because no matter how understanding your husband is, he will never know what it's like to grow up as prey. Not if he's straight and white anyway. He will not know the feeling of car keys clenched between fingers like you learned freshman year of college. He will not know how automatically you cross the street when you're alone to test if that person, that man behind you, is following you or is just going about his business. He will not understand that, sorry, but getting his ass kicked that one time in high school is just not the same as feeling like you alone are in charge of your safety 24/7/365. And that if you step off that path, get drunk, wear a short skirt, leave a party with a boy you just met, were a bitch, were a lesbian, were just not into someone, didn't respond to a catcall, just existed, just breathed, just were a girl, a woman, well, good luck to you.

I need these hot-ass chicks because if there's one thing this world is expert at, it's gaslighting us, it's telling us we're crazy, and honestly it would be no surprise if we actually were. Clearly, we would have reasons.

So: pardon me if by the time we are middle-aged and it seems we are not making enough of an effort to be on proper display while not grossing men out with our very existence and teaching our daughters how not to be assaulted and arranging the magazines on our coffee tables just so, pardon me if I don't get a bit down about how it'd be great to just have a tighter neck or a thinner waist. Because I feel like I'm owed something for having juggled all these chain saws for so long, that all that balancing and "on the other hand"–ing should've resulted in some killer core strength right now. That I should be rewarded with just the right amount of visibility.

I am not asking to be on display, to be open and available to you. I am not asking that you appreciate my eyes or hair or tell me I'm beautiful. I am not asking you to validate anything about me. I've spent my whole life trying to do that, and this is as close as I'll get on that front, I think.

I'm only asking that you don't forget me, don't forget us. Don't forget these hot-ass chicks who have done so much and lived so fast. The ones who have married and birthed and nurtured, the ones who have cried at graves and shrieked at parties. The ones who are being passed over by our culture, our politics, our workplaces, our country. Please don't forget that we love and are loved, that we will scrap with the best of them and oftentimes the worst. Don't make us feel invisible, do not wave your hands through us to see if we're even there.

We are doing and feeding and working and worrying and living and crying and questioning and hooting and loving. Just as we always have.

We are alive; we are living.

And we are here.

We are here.

We are here.

Ashes to Ashes

We had missed her by five minutes.

This woman who always knew where the camera was and would pause midstride to angle her shoulders and flash a smile. This woman who didn't squander a minute or a talent. This woman who was all in—raising children and cherishing grandchildren, working when that wasn't expected, independent yet nurturing, teaching and guiding, ironing every shirt within striking distance, and loving her husband deeply until his last breath, sixty-one years after their wedding day.

For six years we had worried about her mind, her loss. For three years, I felt like every goodbye was The Goodbye. And in the past year, she had retreated almost completely into herself, rarely speaking. But in the end—after all that slow-motion time—the time between the middle-of-the-night call from the nursing home telling us to come back, back down the street, she was getting close, was clearly not enough.

We burst through the door, bleary-eyed and:

"I'm so sorry, she's gone. About five minutes ago."

She was gone. My grandmother was finally, joyfully gone.

Gone from the lack of fresh air and an abundance of confusion. Gone from the most basic of controls over her own body, mind, and routine. Gone from this life that couldn't shake her loose, not just one time but half a dozen times. Gone from an agonizing decline that felt cruel and unending. Gone from us, forever.

My aunt rushed to her side, held her face and touched their foreheads together, tears rushing. After all this, you go out the side door?

Just hours before, exhausted, I had arrived from Vermont and crawled into my grandmother's bed, resting my head on her shoulder. I yawned and felt on the edge of sleep. I felt tears slip across my nose and drop-drop-drop onto my arm. Rolling sadness, relief, and love. I only knew the time based on the blare of her roommate's TV, turned to the evening news. Loud tragedies unfolding everywhere. A quiet mercy slowly unfolding next to me.

———

We sat there, the hallways of the nursing home still. The nurse with the towels and sponge, the surgical gloves, telling us to take our time. The supplies to wash my grandmother's body waiting stacked on the counter.

"I just finished reading a book about funeral homes and death. About how families always used to wash the body themselves, often the women did it. It was no different than taking care of any other family member, like taking care of kids."

My comment hung in the air. More time passed.

I looked over at the stack of supplies; they waited still.

I looked at my aunt. What I was about to suggest making no sense for the person I had always been—the one who was squeamish about everything under the best of circumstances, the one who had to steel herself for morning breath or applying a Band-Aid. The one who felt uncomfortable visiting my grandmother in her last year, not sure how to act, if it was okay to touch her, not wanting to hurt her or misunderstand her or embarrass myself.

This person, me, was the same one who suddenly asked, "Do you think we could help the nurse wash her body?"

Without missing a beat, my aunt Janet replied, "I used to work in a nursing home. I've done this. We could do it."

My uncle Pierre left to get coffee.

The room was quiet, the feeling reverent yet workmanlike.

"I'll do this side, then you do the same thing on her other side," she said.

I was surprised by the smoothness of her skin, especially across her back and legs. She was ninety-three and I had feared what age was already doing to me, never mind what it had done to her. But her body was just a body, like any other body. Her left breast gone but its absence surprisingly not jarring in the least. The surgery scars sprinkled across her body marked every time age or disaster or disease tried to take a swipe at her. They did not mark her deficits; they were a tally of her triumphs.

The warmth of her body a reminder of how close we had been, how close you can be and still miss each other completely. The soapy washcloth gliding across her skin no differently than it would over a baby in a bathtub. You cradle and hold, because the person in your care cannot keep themselves from going under. Rinse the cloth, retrace steps with a clean cloth. Dry.

We paused often to sip coffee from our Dunkin' Donuts cups. On the graveyard shift, we were workers. None of it felt strange. And it felt strange that it didn't feel strange.

When we had to turn her on her side to wash her back, we called in both of my uncles. They tried to absorb what was unfolding as if this wasn't the most out-of-left-field thing that had ever happened. Their mother and mother-in-law had just died, and now here the women were, washing her body, as if Americans did that ever. As if it was no different than any other task, folding laundry, doing the dishes.

Janet tried to instruct them where to hold the sheet my grandmother was lying on but they wanted clearer direction; they wanted to make sure the sheet kept her covered. Things got tense, a little bit, as grief crashed over our task. Everyone sorting and absorbing what this moment meant, unsure what it might mean later. Was this the right thing to do?

Finished, they cleared the soapy towels we had set aside. They left the rest to us. Janet took a sip of her coffee, looked up at me with an arched eyebrow, and under her breath mumbled, "Men."

We both burst out laughing, plumbing the darkness for light.

We rubbed lotion onto her hands and feet, each of us pulling lotion from our handbags to do this. Of course we had lotion in our handbags for just such an occasion, for any occasion. "Women."

My aunt powdered her, just a bit. She clipped a few strands of her bright white angel hair to keep. When the funeral home came for her body, we waited outside and both of my uncles went in. Please make sure she is handled carefully after all of this. After all of this care. After all of this life. She was wrapped in the sheet she had been lying on, lotioned and powdered, and zipped into a gray flannel body bag.

We returned to my aunt and uncle's house around 2:30 a.m., gathered around the dining room table in the dim light, filled short glasses with wine and toasted her. A candle flickered between us on the table. The rest of the world, sound asleep.

I woke up five hours later, feeling relieved.

I woke up five hours later, feeling I had loved and not lost.

I didn't stay much longer after that. The world rushes by,

not caring at all who has gone missing overnight. Life does not wait for the dead and barely pauses for the living. You lose one of the most important people in your life but still there is so much to do.

Back in Vermont, back home, the return to my life felt offensively seamless. I kept forgetting she had died, then I would have to remember it all, all over again. I felt like a disloyal grandchild, an ungrateful human being. The routine of my family and my work swallowed me whole and I was willing to go. I surrendered to the numbness of regular existence.

Five days later, my body surged awake at 2:00 a.m. Life, filling me. The pulse and force of an orgasm, one no one had asked for, filled my consciousness. I plunged my hand under my ratty yoga pants that I had fished out of my bag in the dark the night before, no clean clothes to be found.

My fingers scrambled under my cotton underpants, the ones that were growing snug from the sundaes we were all eating, thanks to the "I Scream for Ice Cream!" basket my son had won at the most recent school fund-raiser.

I expected every ounce of pleasure to dissipate the more awake I became, as it so often did. Dew evaporating in the glare of the early-morning sun.

Instead, it only strengthened. Every slight, quiet movement, another wave. A pit in my stomach. My middle finger slipped farther in, pressing.

I thought of heart valves opening and closing, the elongated shape, the snap-shut of their movements, the electrical impulse. Or the esophagus, swallowing, pink and shiny in the glare of a surgical light. This body of openings, of closings, of pathways ignored until they require attention.

I thought of the first time I had fingers inside of me. We parked in his car after school, on a back road near my house. His car, a half-rusted boat, pulled into a turnoff under enormous pines. Needles fell from the branches and hit, marking our time.

My bra unhooked, my shirt not even off, no one had time for that. Pants unzipped and shoved down. I thought about how everything we do out of necessity when we're young becomes something we need to role-play at twenty or thirty years later. When you always have access to a bed and nothing but permission? Spare me. You want to get caught, have no time, who cares if we're comfortable? Wanting to feel, touch, the pull-off on a dirt road, the driveway of your parents' house after a party, it never seemed easy, did it? You had to want it, even if you didn't know exactly what *it* was.

I thought of him dropping me off after that, still in the bright light of the afternoon, I walked our dogs, the ache I felt from realizing there was an inside to me, exciting, new. Things were different now, my head pinballing. Each step I took, the ache, a reminder.

I thought of the first boy I had sex with, who upon finding out I was a virgin made it his unspoken mission to make me not a virgin. He taught me how melting it was to plunge your tongue into someone else's ear and how hot breath can make you feel like you've left your body behind. He also taught me what it's like to be used and discarded, by dropping me cold the day after we had sex. No phone calls, no notes, no nothing.

I guess it must be hard to be a big fish in a shallow puddle, watching all your contemporaries move on and have a life. And there you are, feeling the need to dip deeper and deeper into the pool of younger and younger girls to stay relevant. Although you graduated from high school already. Although you were once so cool. And here I am, all these years later, still utterly devoid of sympathy. Sad face.

I shifted my weight, and pressed harder into my hand, another wave.

I thought, *It's officially Mother's Day right now, and I have to even do this shit for myself.*

I thought of the soccer player I had sex with the night of my high school graduation party. He had moved to our town for the summer with his college roommate, a graduate of our high school. He was from England and that accent, Jesus Christ. In our rural Massachusetts, dull-as-shit, white-bread town, here was—well, let's face it—another white guy. But with an accent! It honestly didn't take much.

I never felt good enough for any of the boys in my high school, most of them made sure of that. Not intentionally, not in a cruel way, but in a way that said, "You are literally the only girl in your social circle we have not dated." But this outsider, this genuine alien to our town, this athletic fox, somehow felt differently. And he felt differently in front of all of them.

It's not like I suddenly became the prom queen, it wasn't quite that big, but it was enough. Fuck you, everyone! People see something in me; *he* sees something in me. We didn't date, not officially, because that would've been too much. Too visible, too much of an endorsement, too satisfying. But we were together that summer. I'd pick him up from work and we would lounge in my car with the windows down, the lush chirping of the thick summer air surrounding us.

He ran his hands over my bare breasts, down my stomach, and said, "You have a beautiful body." No one had ever said that to me before. I'm not sure anyone has said it since. But maybe I just stopped listening a long time ago.

I thought of the one boyfriend I had in high school who saw me, really saw me. Saw how I was different, saw who I could be, would be. I'm not even sure *boyfriend* is the right term; it was so fast, our timing off. But I can still remember, thirty years later, parking in his car (there were so many cars) and how good he smelled. I remember his winter scarf and burying my face in it, inhaling. I remember my best friend and I debating, could it be cologne or was it just the laundry detergent his mom used? I still don't know. I should ask him.

I thought of the blur of one-night stands and early-twenties really terrible decisions. A long-haired bartender in a pool in Dallas. A client from work who I straddled in public at a shitty bar down the street from my shitty apartment. The barback from the college bar my best friend and I practically lived at; he would sometimes come over after his shift. The next time I saw him, a lifetime later, he was in the "Hot Issue" of *Rolling Stone*. I thought of the apartments I snuck out of and the people I cheated on or with. I thought of the rug burns and the flowers, the hangovers and the regrets. I thought of the few moments of tenderness. I thought of tall blond Anton who drove a Saab, who had to be almost ten years older than me. The one my roommates and I giggled over and called A Real Man, the shock of his attractiveness in general and attraction to me specifically never went away.

I remember being so drunk one night that a guy I had met in a bar started to fuck me in his bed even though I was passed out and I woke up, into it enough. Only after he was almost done did I realize his roommate was still in the room, wide-awake, watching. They both knew he was watching. They had probably planned it. I really didn't care.

I thought of the thirty-two-year-old I was dating when I was seventeen; I can still remember the monochromatic outfit I wore to the winter carnival dance that night, a blue satin dress with blue stockings—a fashion tip from a mall store, one I might add, that's surprisingly spot-on all these years later. How I went to his house afterward, how he ran his hands under my dress and up my back, how he stuck his fingers inside me while we stood, while I pressed into him. It never went further than that.

He would call me at home to see if I could go away with him on a business trip and I'd have to say, "I can't, I have school."

My husband woke up, shifted, got up, and went to the bathroom. I lay there, still. My breath shallow. An alligator at the surface of the water, eyes fixed.

This wasn't something I wanted anyone else to finish.

An hour had already passed.

I thought of flirting and how much I miss the real thing. The real kind that could lead somewhere. I wonder, *What would his hair feel like between my fingers and how would he kiss?* I don't think of fucking anyone else or having affairs, not often anyway. It just feels like a lot of work, navigating each other's issues and likes and hang-ups. I would just like to kiss more, different people, to remember what being surprised feels like. To remember what different feels like.

I have been at weddings and funerals, kids' birthday parties and high school reunions, and inevitably I end up in a conversation with someone I have kissed, a long time ago.

Sometimes it was more than that.

We'll sit there with a drink in our hands and talk about how life is going or how our jobs or kids are and at some point I will inevitably think, *You once had your penis in my vagina. And we both know it. You went down on me, I can still see you. I can still taste you.* And depending on how long the drinking goes on, there is always an exchange of looks that verifies, yes, we both know it. We have not forgotten.

I thought of how I never once had sex throughout my pregnancy with my son. I was so afraid of doing anything at all to jeopardize it after having had a miscarriage the year before. And I thought of how I had sex constantly when I was pregnant with my daughter, how blood surged through me and I would wake up in the middle of the night, needing it.

I thought of when my husband and I got engaged and we went down to our local bar to celebrate (automatically I now think, *What did we do with the kids?* So foreign is the idea of utter and complete freedom without coverage and favors.) And I immediately launched into, "Well, you should probably know everyone I slept with, because a bunch of them will be at our wedding."

I thought about how he didn't even flinch.

I thought of my husband's hands, big and rough. I thought of his ability to cry, easily. I thought of him not being even a little bit squeamish about periods or having to unclog a toilet I myself have clogged. I thought of love and what that even means anymore, twenty years in. I thought of all the ways I have not deserved it. I thought of all the ways I still do. I thought of how I want to be surprised and loved, grabbed and taken. Flirted with, shamelessly. Cared for, endlessly.

Another hour, gone.

My left arm was numb from laying down on it. I slowly pulled my fingers out and they were pruned from being wet for so long. I felt the ridges on them, the dampness of my clothes, the faint smell of fresh sweat on my skin.

The birds started to chirp, the faint inky blue of the coming morning. Mother's Day.

I thought, I have pushed so many of these thoughts down. I

have given up so much of what sent blood coursing through my body from the time I was thirteen. I have suppressed the feeling of wrapping my arms around a jean jacket and kissing under a streetlight, tasting a freshly smoked cigarette on someone else's mouth.

I have pushed away the notion I am still alive, I have given myself over to raising children and feeling professionally fulfilled and having opinions on The Issues. I have forgotten what it feels like to live and die on a comment, a call, a hand lightly brushing against my arm. The body electric, always lying in wait.

I thought, in the last hour of this full body rebellion, this reunion of musky memory, *Am I returning?*

Did I return from a death to get back to my life?

I thought, *Maybe I'm only halfway through my days.*

I thought, *Why am I giving up on myself so soon?*

I thought, *I am not ash.*

Not yet.

TIME-OUT

Fifty-One Things You Should Never Say to a Mother Ever

1. "Your daughter is so beautiful!"
   So you're saying she's dumb.

2. "Your daughter is so smart!"
   So you're saying she's ugly.

3. "So great how you give him so much freedom."
   So you're saying I neglect him.

4. "He's really lucky to have a parent who's so attentive!"
   So you're saying I smother him.

5. "Hello!"
   Racist.

6. "How are you?"
   Doesn't recognize the struggle.

7. "Would you like a refill on that coffee?"
   starts sobbing

8. "Boarding pass, please."
   Isn't that so like you.

9. " The weather this afternoon at San Francisco International
   Airport is sixty-three degrees and foggy."
   I CAN'T EVEN.

10. "I haven't seen you in so long, you've obviously been busy!"
    You did not just.

11. "You look tired."
    Oh my God.

12. "You look great!"
    Oh my God.

13. "Your son knows more about computers than I do!"
    *So you're saying my house is a hedonistic den of screen
    time.*

14. "I wish my daughter liked being outside as much as your
    daughter does."
    *So you're saying she's doomed to die penniless and
    alone because she doesn't know how to code.*

15. "How can I help?"
    So you're saying I look like I need help.

16. "Can I get you anything at the store?"
    So you're saying I look like I'm out of everything.

17. "Would your kids like to come with us to go get ice cream?"
    *So you're saying I look like I'm anti-ice-cream-at-
    home.*

18. "How was your summer?"
    I cried a lot?

19. "Oh, two, four, and six are such great ages!"
    Ma'am, don't mock me.

20. "It gets easier!"
    HOW DARE YOU.

21. "Looks like you have your hands full!"
    I SAID HOW DARE YOU.

22. "Such a beautiful day, isn't it?"
    I JUST.

23. "Merry Christmas!"
    SERIOUSLY, GO FUCK YOURSELF.

24. "This coffee cake is delicious!"
    So you're saying I like missionary in particular.

25. "I love what you've done with your house!"
    Feminism just called, it said it's dead. The funeral is at three.

26. "How long have you been breastfeeding?"
    Long enough to know this is a trick question.

27. "It's fine to give your baby a bottle—don't listen to those nursing Nazis."
    starts sobbing

28. "Your husband is such a good dad!"

    Yeah, men tend to really shine at about the 35 percent parenting level.

29. "Being a mother is hard."

    So you're saying I make it look not easy.

30. "Being a mother is a gift."

    Where's my receipt?

31. "Being a mother is the best job there is."

    And the profit sharing? Oooh hoo boy.

32. "Being a mother is thankless."

    Am I talking to myself again? I am, I can tell.

33. "He's an angel."

    Don't tell me, you're a grandmother?

34. "He's an angel sent straight from heaven!"

    I told you to stay out of this, Holly Hunter.

35. "Can I take your order?"

    starts sobbing

36. "Would you like a dressing room?"

    Yes, because I would like to threaten my children in private.

37. "How's it going in there?"

    YOU KNOW HOW IT'S GOING IN HERE.

38. "Need any other sizes?"

    If you say, "Bigger," I WILL STUFF THIS
    SWEATER DOWN MY PANTS.

39. "Thank you!"

    Wow.

40. "Please come again!"

    Can you even hear yourself?

41. "Would you like to take it for a test drive?"

    Off a cliff with you in it, yes.

42. "Or should we wait for your husband?"

    To knee you square in the 1950s? No, I can do that
    myself.

43. "So how did it handle?"

    The thing is just so well honed. Not only is its
    electrically assisted steering system unexpectedly
    sensitive, you can practically feel the thousands of
    man-hours spent developing its Michelin tires, its
    stiffer structure and, on Z51 models, its electronically
    controlled limited-slip differential. Even on narrower
    rubber, the C7 has grip figures on par with the
    outgoing Z06. Okay, fine, I got that from Car and
    Driver.

44. "Wow, he's gotten so tall!"

    So you're saying he's too big for his age.

45. "Oh my gosh, look at those tiny feet."
    So you're saying she's too small for her age.

46. "Look at that belly!"
    I hope you're talking about my kid.

47. "Look at that naked bummy!"
    Seriously, please be talking about my ki— WHY ARE
    YOU NAKED RIGHT NOW? YOU'RE TWELVE.

48. "Look at you all together, what a beautiful family."
    starts sobbing

49. "Did you see that movie that just came out?"
    I don't know, was it called Fuck Me for Having
    Friends Who Have a Life?

50. "Did you read that new book?"
    *Mmmmm, busy doing a little something over
    here called* HELPING THE HUMAN RACE
    CONTINUE. *Now if you'll excuse me, I need to get
    back up on my cross.*

51. "Don't you ever wonder what that sweet baby is thinking?"
    Oh, I know exactly what he's thinking: I hate
    everyone.

Is There a Parenting Expert on This Plane?

Ladies and gentlemen, this is your captain speaking. We're now at a cruising altitude of thirty thousand feet and I've turned off the fasten-seat-belt sign. Feel free to get up, stretch your legs, and move about the cabin. Also, while I have your attention, it seems there's a child in 9D who is completely incapable of spreading cream cheese onto his bagel by himself and there's growing concern in that section of the aircraft that he doesn't have enough "grit."

Is there a parenting expert on this plane?

Great, the flight attendant is telling me 153 of you are. She also mentioned that his mother didn't raise her hand. Interesting.

Look, today it's cream cheese, tomorrow it's not being able to slather lubricant on an ultrasound wand. It's just never too early for the general public—specifically white men in positions of power—to step in and tell women they're so very wrong and to detail all the ways they're so very wrong. I also find it never hurts (me) to explain things to them in a way I might to a small child. Mom, would you like a pair of pilot wings? No, no, I insist.

Quick show of hands, how many of you believe 9D can't spread his big-baby cream cheese due to the fact his mother doesn't allow him to free-range enough, and by "enough" I mean an acceptable amount according to strangers on the playground, neighbors, and those of us heading to Chicago this afternoon—

where the weather is a mild seventy-two degrees and it's partly cloudy—none of whom know this family personally?

I'm being told 148. Yes, that's what I was afraid of.

Is there a Tiger Mom in the house? Anyone raise their kid in France? Any kids on board who manage their parents' finances— hold on, I'm being told that the boy in 9D is four years old and this is his first time flying. And now I'm getting a message from the control tower . . . yup, yup. Got it . . . okay, they said and I quote, "Oh boo-hoo, sounds like the excuses of someone who will never be able to hold down a job or find happiness in the arms of a life partner." They also suggested I put my fists up at the outer corners of my eyes and curl them in and out to make the internationally recognized sign of the crybaby, like this. But, hey, by all means, 9D's mom, keep spreading his cream cheese for him. *Jesus.*

I mean, who am I? Just some "guy" who holds all your lives in his extremely independent, staying-dry-at-night, spreadin'-cream-cheese-all-by-himself hands.

Look, no one has time for this, 9D. It's time you put your big boy pants on and change the oil on your mom's car when you get home.

WHAT DO YOU MEAN YOU DON'T KNOW HOW? That's it. I've had enough of this.

DOES ANYONE KNOW HOW TO FLY A PLANE?

The cocaptain. Of course, apologies . . . Please take over, Todd.

Ladies and gentlemen, this is your captain speaking from in front of you right now, in the middle of the aisle. The flight attendants will be starting beverage service soon and I suggest you order a double because we've got some serious meddling and undermining to do.

Look, how can we get 9D to step it up over here? Feel free to just shout out your craziest, most judgmental thoughts.

"Tell the boy's mother everything she's doing wrong but also get something in there about cherishing every moment, it goes by so fast, et cetera, et cetera, et cetera." Yes, good, good.

"Look on disapprovingly, no matter what's happening." Well, that certainly is a timeless one!

"Diagnose the child even though I work in a bank. Perhaps suggest 9D is autistic and ask the mother if she ever saw Claire Danes in that Temple Grandin movie because it was marvelous." Creative, cultural, and on trend, I really like where you're going with that one.

"Just sigh a lot and act exasperated, as though I myself was never a small child who had to learn self-control and life skills. And then pivot to add a dig in there like 'I suppose you're one of those working mothers who has someone else raising her kid for her? Because it obviously shows.' Something like that." Perhaps a bridge too far, but interesting. Okay, food for thought.

Another quick show of hands, will this child eventually be able to spread cream cheese on his own simply by maturing and learning skills at his own pace?

Two. What are you even thinking, 23A? And mom to 9D, please stay out of this.

Or will he only be able to get a grip if his mother quits her job and commits to being at home full-time, which is the natural habitat for those of you with vaginas "who've been through the wringer"?

152. Yes, thank you. THANK YOU.

Last, are we helping or hurting?

One vote for hurting, 152 for helping. Hold up, the one vote for hurting is from the boy's mother. Ma'am, I said stay out of this.

Look, if there's one thing I think we can all agree on, it's that all of us—except one—are right. No one knows what's better for a child than someone who has precious little information about that child or his circumstances. Bonus points if it's been at least three decades since you've parented a young child yourself. Double bonus points if you've never had any children at all.

Who's with me on this?

First class, I CAN'T HEAR YOU!

Very last row in front of the bathrooms, HOLLA! Oopsie daisy, apparently that made 9D cry. Well, that's hardly surprising, is it?

Everyone in coach, LET ME HEAR YOU SCREAM!

FREEDOMS

Do You Have Faith in Me?

"Do you have faith in me?!" My daughter shout-asked from across the skate park. She stood there, helmet and pads on, never having been on a skateboard before, opting for a scooter at this birthday party, as she considered going down a small ramp.

"Do you have faith in me?" she repeated, this girl who is nothing if not supremely confident. In just a six-word question she summed up the last eleven years of my life, of trying to control my worry, my anxiety, real anxiety, to have faith. In me. In them. In the world.

For me, raising children has been one long strength-building exercise in self-control. Not the kind of self-control that really matters—I yell, throw tantrums, slam my fist down on the table when everything's unraveling. But the kind of control it takes to keep my anxiety wrestled into a submissive position, to remind myself tragedy isn't the only option, to attempt to hide from them I'm worried. I'm always worried.

Becoming a mother made my anxiety—a thing I never really thought I had—explode into a Technicolor display of irrational imagination. In just the sixty seconds it took me to hustle down to our roadside mailbox and back, I imagined in graphic detail how it had been just enough time for our two lazy dogs to rip my infant son apart, to pull him from his cushion-enclosed nap spot on the couch and devour him in a feeding frenzy. It was the thing that made every trip to a playground, bike path, or pool one long stress test for me, cringing and shouting, "Be careful!" But it never inoculated them from anything. Not her falling from the monkey bars in a position that can only be described as "invisible chair," when I thought she had broken her tailbone. It didn't inoculate him from choking on pool water, or either of them from falling—on their teeth, on the side of their heads, on their knees. It never protected them from anything; it never saved us a single trip to the ER.

When my son was six, he was diagnosed with generalized anxiety disorder as a free gift with purchase with his Asperger's diagnosis. As parents (as humans) we're very quick to say so, okay, that's *you*. That's *your* thing. We should definitely, definitely work on that. It took me a while to realize, wait, hold up, I think that actually might be *my* thing too.

I slowly began to trace the web backward. My shyness as a kid and, to a lesser degree, as an adult. My fear of speaking up, of saying the wrong thing, of saying anything in certain situations. My fear of hurting myself—I have clear memories of inching my way down our hill in winter to get to the school bus stop, careful to avoid the patches of ice hiding under the snow, waiting to betray me. It's why I don't ski, snowboard, mountain bike, and barely know how to swim. I've never plunged into a pool, jumped from a boat into a lake. The risks I take are creative and mostly theoretical. They are never physical. And when I thought I had a handle on it, had named it, or at least understood it was there, like a disloyal shadow, it turned on me.

Last September I prepared to get up in front of eighty people—the most open, supportive, enthusiastic eighty people possible—and make a brief ten-minute announcement. That's it. That's all. But the longer the first speakers took, the more I felt my nerves suddenly ramp up. My legs felt a little weak, my heart about to explode. I told myself that this was just normal nervousness for me. I always felt nervous before speaking or presenting, but once I got up there and got rolling, I'd be fine. Well, more or less fine. I'd be mostly fine. Plus, I had no idea what actually existed beyond normal nervousness.

But in what felt like a flash, my run-of-the-mill nervousness crossed a hard line it had never, not once, crossed before. I imagined what walking up to the front of the room would feel like, and I was pretty sure it would feel like walking through oatmeal while wearing cement shoes. I felt my legs about to buckle. I didn't faint, and although I had never fainted before, I was sure this must be what it felt like. My chest tightened. I wasn't sure my legs actually even worked anymore. I couldn't imagine opening my mouth and anything coming out of it except moths and cotton. And in that instant it all came crashing down—I lurched over to my partner in this project, a partner not prepared to speak at all, threw her my notes and said, "I have to go," and walked out the side door just as my introduction was happening.

It felt as fucked-up, awful, and upsetting as you might imagine. I felt freaked-out. I felt wildly unprofessional. I felt like an utter loser. I really didn't know what had happened. I still don't know what happened. A panic attack, I guess. My first.

Maybe I wasn't eating enough, not enough protein; I wasn't sleeping a lot on that trip; we all drank together the night before; maybe I was dehydrated. I reasoned I had become either too comfortable or too lazy about rehearsing, something I had relied on previously to feel prepared and confident. I had underestimated I would need to do that in this situation too. I hadn't taken it seriously nor prepared as I might otherwise, since this was supposed to be easy, quick, and casual. That's what everyone told me. I told myself that was the full story as well as the end of it. Just an anomaly.

But two months later I was in a meeting, a routine mundane

meeting, and as we went around to introduce ourselves, the longer it took to get to me the more nervous I felt, and as soon as I thought, *I hope what happened in September isn't happening again*, I triggered it. I made it through, the thought of the humiliation greater than the anxiety, but barely. My face was hot; I felt like I was speaking from under water. Sweat prickled all over my body, and the taste of metal flashed in my mouth. No one could have known I'd been seconds from fleeing, from passing out, from wanting out. Here, keep your money.

I don't know what's happening, this anxiety that reshapes in me every ten or twenty years. I don't know why this fear of the physical is now exploding into a fear of the interpersonal, the mundane, into the part of the world I felt like I had a handle on. I can trigger it the way you can conjure pain by pressing on a bruise or feel the electric zing of a loose tooth by pushing it with your tongue. I test it. Which seems unwise, but frankly, I'm pissed about it. I didn't do anything you didn't want me to do and now you want to take even more away from me? I didn't take risks, I kept myself safe, I've worked completely under the radar and this is the thanks I get? Fuck you, anxiety.

We always think we're alone in our misery, don't we? We think we're so special as to have problems and ailments that only we have experienced. We all think we're the next subjects of the Diagnosis column in the *New York Times*.

But every time I reveal something of myself, take the risk in asking a friend, "Has this ever happened to you?" the answer is almost always a shy, quiet yes. Miscarriage? Yes. Financial freak-outs? Yes. Panic attacks? Yup. We're so afraid of failure. And anxiety feels like one long fucking failure.

I've learned over time to avoid some of the situations where I'll hold my kids back, where I'll be nothing but a chorus of be-carefulbecarefulbecareful. Those are the things my husband fields, where he lets them be kids and take risks and get hurt and get back up again. They know I'm the Parent Who Worries. I don't think they understand the true extent of it, but maybe I'm just being naive. Because by the time my daughter was four and I shouted, "Please be careful, watch what you're doing!" as she scrambled up and over a rock embankment near the lake she quietly replied down to the sand, "Mom, I'll be fine. Don't worry."

Don't worry.

As my children get older, more capable, I find myself loosening up. Maybe that's why my anxiety is now pointing inward, at myself, instead of outward at them. My son has pushed past and learned to control so much of the anxiety that crippled him when he was little. But if I've learned anything, anxiety is as adaptable as a virus. It will be with him, always. Even he understands this. So why can't I?

Maybe that's why my daughter's question rang out so clearly to me, hitting me square. I can still hear it ringing out. It's a question I've started asking myself.

"Do you have faith in me?"

"I do!" I yelled back in response to this question she had never, not once, asked me before. Tears leaped to my eyes, no one around us grasping the explosion of meaning in our exchange.

A girl who scooted past her, a girl she had never met before shouted, "I HAVE FAITH IN YOU!" and that seemed to mean just as much as my reply.

She asked one last time, "Do you have faith in me?!"

I shouted back "I do!" and the scooter girl zipped between us again and repeated, "I HAVE FAITH IN YOU!"

Do you have faith in me, I do, I have faith in you. This circle so snug between the three of us. A mother, a daughter, a peer. In that moment, the balance so exquisite between what our parents tell us and what our peers encourage. How they become equal, one meaning as much as the other, even if that peer is a stranger. How the people who know us the least are sometimes just as much a vote of confidence as those who know us best. The people who know us well, giving us too much leeway, maybe support and feed our fears too much. The people who don't know us, believing anything is possible, push us and make us brave.

We need both.

I repeat this to myself now, in a round. In those moments, the moments when I worry, the moments when I wonder, *Is this happening again? Could the worst happen?* I think, *Do you have faith in me?*

I do.

I have faith in you.

Thirteen with Dudes

If you have camped more than once, then you have had a best-worst camping trip. A best-worst camping trip is when everything somehow went wrong and right, where you were close to pulling the rip cord on the whole thing but then were rewarded handsomely for staying the course. Maybe it started out with having to tarp an entire site and set up two tents in a crashing thunderstorm, as my husband and kids had to just a few weeks ago—finally retreating to the truck when it all became too unmanageable, too terrifying, and too swear-y. How would I know if I wasn't there? Because these details—especially the swearing details—were the first things my kids blurted out when they busted through the door that Sunday afternoon.

Regardless, sometimes thunderstorms give way to vivid rainbows seen in full, or a gorgeous afternoon of jumping off docks and lazy canoeing, or maybe an after-lunch nap in a shaded tent, skin warm and fragrant from sunscreen, piney bug spray, and sweat. And sometimes your worst moment is almost getting into a fist fight with people twenty years younger than you only to tumble straight into the best idea in the entirety of the parenting canon.

On this particular trip, we were camping at Burton Island State Park, an idyllic spot on an actual island in Lake Champlain. Meaning, you need to take a ferry there; meaning, you can't just fill your car up to the rearview mirror with your crap and let it explode at your campsite; meaning, this park is in such high demand everyone reserves prime sites the year before and might be a bit amped by the time they get there, weighed down with bags and bikes and beer.

Our campsite was tucked into the woods, with that elusive balance of shade and sunlight, and with a clear view of the lake across the path from us. We also had a view of all the lucky bastards who had reserved the lakefront sites and lean-tos, close enough to hear the teeny-tiny lake waves lap at the rocks and exposed tree roots. I imagined them all being logged into the state parks reservations systems at midnight the day the sites came online. I admired them and hated them in equal measure.

Our site was also located entirely too close—really, within punching distance—to a group of twentysomething fuckheads who only grew in number, dogs, and tequila as the night wore on. We overenthusiastically engaged our kids in conversation for the sole purpose of distracting them from the Kid Rock cruise-on-land that was unfolding next to us.

Our kids were eight and ten, and for some reason I felt like that was maybe a little too young to have to hear a bunch of dipshits and their chorus of simple sentences that were mostly constructed as such: subject + *fucking* + verb + *fucking* + direct object. We kept them up late, knowing there was nothing regular about a regular bedtime in this situation. Besides, we hoped the late night would push them over the edge sleepiness-wise and allow them to crash even though they were only separated from Dumbassmageddon by a thin nylon barrier.

Jon and I kept drinking, in the hopes it would also send us into a dead sleep. But mostly what it did was simultaneously take the edge off while creating new, different edges. The kind of edges attached to knife handles. We hated every single human being at that campsite. Like an old movie, the clock hands whirled fast past 9:00 p.m., then past quiet hours at 10:00 p.m., 11:00 p.m., OH MY GOD, MIDNIGHT, HOW MUCH DO WE HAVE TO DRINK TO MAKE THIS END?

Finally, my nonconfrontational husband teetered over to their site with his headlamp on and his millionth beer in hand. It took him maybe five steps total to get there. Pretty sure when he got there one of the guys was slapping a girl's ass as they all hooted and hollered. I hate people.

He piped up with a "Guys. It's midnight. My kids are asleep. They've had to listen to you swearing and screaming all night. Can you wrap it up?"

One loudmouth said something back that I think contained vowels and consonants but mostly just sounded like Barney from *The Simpsons*. Jon came back. They started to break it up, meaning not go to bed but just take their booze and go to the edge of the water or up to the meadow, and I wouldn't have cared if they went to Mars as long as they got the hell away from us.

We stayed by our fire for another few minutes, enjoying the break in our jaw-clenching battle of livers. In an attempt to stop fantasizing about shooting flaming arrows at their campsite, I noticed that the lakefront campsites and lean-tos across from us seemed to be occupied by one giant group. All of the adults over there were also still up, around their huge campfire. There were tons of kids—so many kids—now all asleep in their tents.

When we had set up earlier that day, there were teenagers standing on the roofs of the lean-tos armed with Super Soakers and younger kids plastering themselves up against trees and tents, trying not to be seen. All-out war was constantly raging across at least six campsites, it was a borderless, lawless country. We were hemmed in by dipshits to the left and a sovereign nation in front of us. On a friggin' island no less.

A few things about this sovereign nation had caught my eye

however. I thought back and realized the kids were a crazy range of ages, from maybe seven years old all the way up to teenagers and even college kids. Everyone gathered for meals, got ready for bed, brushed teeth, and set out for the day together. Kayaking, swimming, whatever, it was done in a group. It wasn't just one endless *Lord of the Flies* over there. Sure, it looked like that initially, but there was definitely a method to the madness.

And, above all else, the kids were really nice. I didn't totally approve of them tromping all over the roofs of the lean-tos, because come *on*. But when my son stood at the end of our campsite's pathetic little dirt path and stared longingly at all the fun they were having, two of the teenage kids—not the youngest kids, but teenagers!—came over and said, "Hey, buddy, do you want to play?" and brought him into the fold.

Something was going on. Something was . . . off. But somehow something was very, very right.

Like a dope slap to the side of the head I whipped around to my husband and said, "THERE ARE NO MOMS ON THAT CAMPING TRIP OVER THERE." And he looked at me, surveyed the scene, and laughed, "Holy shit, you're RIGHT." Suddenly the absence of nagging, assorted soul-crushing instructions, and general fun-killing finally made sense. Not to mention all that fearless scaling of lean-tos. But those kids were *happy*. They were free and wild, yet not given a free pass to act like jerks, unlike the shitheads next to us.

"You should do that. You should have a camping trip like that."

The very next summer, that's exactly what Jon did with our other dad friends and their kids. And Dad Camp was officially born. On Father's Day weekend no less.

I can't speak to the particulars of what unfolded over that first weekend, because they were not shared with me. I knew not to ask too many questions, one, because I wouldn't get many answers, and, two, because I didn't really care. The kids were gone, I had a weekend to myself, and everyone came home on Sunday. What's to know?

But the thing about kids who aren't teenagers yet is they will gladly narc on their dad given the slightest opportunity. Every year I've heard about which dads got in trouble with the park rangers and at least a handful of things they were specifically told "not to tell the moms." Kids are double agents, man; you can't ever trust them.

But what I do know, from stories and videos and the random grab bag of photos I've seen over the past few years, is by the end of that weekend there is one big bonded pack of filthy, happy kids. And another big bonded pack of relaxed—and also filthy and happy—dads. Dad Camp is the younger version of the sovereign nation we witnessed on that best-worst camping trip. The youngest campers have been just two or three years old, and my son has always been the oldest, now at thirteen. They've dug in the clay at the edge of the water, wolfed down chocolate chip pancakes from the one dad who made those his specialty (and by default ended up feeding breakfast to every single kid on the trip). They've canoed and kayaked, gathered around campfires and smacked each other with pool noodles. All without a "Now what do you say?" or a "Be careful!" or a "Are you hungry?"

They eat when the food is ready. They go brush their teeth when our friend Eric takes out his guitar and leads them in a toothbrushing song he makes up on the spot. This was such a big hit the first year a park ranger noticed and asked him if he would come back and perform at the state park. He declined, but it was a testament to the spirit this big pack of dads and kids brought to the trip (and to Eric's talent, enthusiasm, and improv abilities, of course).

Typically at some point a group photo is taken. All the dads. All the kids. Usually it's raining. When I saw the group photo from the inaugural Dad Camp my first thought was, *These are good men.*

I have thought it every year since.

My eyes scan their faces and I see creative directors and professors, musicians and marketers, a carpenter, writers. For some, that weekend is just one in a series of camping trips they'll pack into that summer. For others, it's the one time they'll camp all year. Every single one of these men is a good husband, a great father, a stellar human being. They are involved in their children's lives in ways mundane and profound; this trip being just one in a myriad of ways they model what fatherhood looks like now. They model what it should've looked like all along.

They are involved. They are capable. They are smart and funny and let the kids be the unruly creatures they're meant to be.

This year, Dad Camp fell not only on Father's Day weekend, as it usually does, but also on my son's thirteenth birthday. I am a serious birthday person. Not in the way that I go overboard when it comes to birthdays—although I sometimes do—but in the way that I clear everything from my calendar for my kids' birthdays. Even when I was working full-time I made sure to take the day off.

This tradition actually started with me, well before I had kids. All because one day, while I worked on my birthday, I came dangerously close to calling a client a cunt on a conference call. In my defense, she really was a cunt. But it seemed to me if I was expecting other humans to be especially nice and deferential to me on my birthday, work was not the place to spend my day.

From that moment on I always took my birthday off. And once I became a freelancer? Hell, I'd take the whole week (month?) off. Your birthday is your Birth Day, people. If you're not gonna celebrate the hell out of it, then who will?

Your mom, that's who. That's why I carried my tradition over to their birthdays. They're both summer babies, so I never had to contend with getting them out of school (but trust me, I would have). But this? I wasn't really prepared for this.

For about six and a half minutes I entertained heading out to their campsite and bringing an ice cream cake. Then I thought about the logistics, how they'd need to definitely be there when I arrived or the cake would melt, how it'd be disruptive to their whole day. I thought about how terrible the reception was out there, how easily something intended to be simple could turn into a frustrating pain in the ass for everyone. But finally what dawned on me was the fact that my son was turning thirteen.

Thirteen.

He was going to be a teenager. As silly as this will sound, I was sort of stunned to realize we wouldn't always be spending his birthday together. I wouldn't always clear that day in my calendar, we wouldn't always go out to breakfast or to the granite quarry or a baseball game. We wouldn't go to McDonald's for fries and shakes (or as I like to call it, the Vegetarian Special). We wouldn't plan to haunt construction sites or watch farmers haying or go for ice cream afterward. There wouldn't be bowling parties or swimming. There wouldn't even be cake together or a pile of presents wrapped in goofy wrapping paper. There wouldn't be any need for me to arrange anything to do with his birthday, never mind plan an entire day.

Recovering, I decided to just let his birthday be his birthday. For the first time, without me.

Instead, he would turn thirteen with a bunch of dudes. It suddenly seemed more than a compromise; it seemed like the most fitting turn of events. On Day One of his teenage years, he would be surrounded by men modeling how to be a good man. How to be capable and strong, how to be independent and encouraging, and above all, how to have fun without fear. He knew most of these men since he was young enough to remember things and has admired many of them for their senses of humor, their musical chops, their inappropriate jokes, and their adventurous spirits.

You could do worse on your thirteenth birthday. You could be with your mom as she demands you wear a button-down shirt to a fancy breakfast.

I asked for their help, I asked them to be my surrogates. I asked them to remember their thirteen-year-old selves, to give him advice, to just help him have a happy birthday. Sure, I was met with the level of smart-assery I'd come to expect, like offers to bring their old *Playboys* along as well as some outlining of male rites of passage (drinking cow's blood, waking at dawn), but underneath it all every response told me, "Of course. We've got this."

The weekend passed in radio silence. No texts, no calls, no FaceTiming, no nothing. My son had left as a twelve-year-old, would return as a thirteen-year-old, and I hadn't even called him to wish him a happy birthday. I hadn't hugged him or lit a single candle. His presents awaited him on the dining room table, in a house filled with silence. I pressed my girlfriends into service: "I will cry all day if we don't do something." We had cocktails in the afternoon, went to see *Wonder Woman*, stayed up too late drinking whiskey and telling secrets from our own teenage years. It felt like the beginning of my life fully becoming mine again. Even if for one night, even just for the weekend. I could see it.

When they returned that Sunday, the regular rituals held. They were filthy and happy. They needed to shower, and everything they brought with them—pillows, sleeping bags, sneakers—needed to be washed. In hot water. They were full of stories (although they saved the narcing for Monday morning when Jon left for work. *They grow up so fast*).

Jon had brought a bunch of cupcakes for Walker's birthday, and it turned out my son shared his birthday with another boy on the trip. So there were lots of cupcakes and candles, singing and gorging. It was not fancy. It was great. No one overthought it. No one belabored it.

I thought back to that best-worst camping trip, when I had given the kids permission to make as much noise as they wanted when they rose at 6:00 a.m. It was a delicious form of payback to our still sleeping—and undoubtedly excruciatingly hungover—neighbors (I may have provided pots, pans, and wooden spoons to amplify their efforts).

And I thought of the sovereign nation across from us as they slowly emerged from their tents. The campfire roaring again, coffee being made by and for tired (and also hungover) dads. Bowls of cereal and egg sandwiches being distributed as everyone huddled around a picnic table or the fire. A community like any community, but this one just happened to be bound by fresh air and Super Soakers.

While Jon slept, I walked to the campground store to get a coffee, my kids racing ahead of me on their bikes. We had already been up far too long and coffee couldn't wait. The damp coolness of the early morning was quickly giving way to another blazing summer day.

We exited the wider path leading to the store, passing the freestanding payphone where we stopped to take photos. Something so standard in my youth, now a hands-on-hips curiosity for my kids. As we got closer to the store I looked over to one of the picnic tables, where two of the girls from the tequila-soaked fuckfest sat. Sunglasses firmly on, they were hunched over and clutching their cups of campground-store coffee as if they were life rafts.

We poked around the store, this was always one of my favorite parts about camping or vacationing somewhere remote and near water. How the overabundance of choice we live with every day as Americans is whittled down to this reduction sauce of vacation necessity—lures and doughnuts, local newspapers and firewood. Matches, fishing line, jugs of water, butter and eggs, ice cream sandwiches, citronella candles, aloe and sunscreen, candy bars and aluminum foil. We need so little to get by yet convince ourselves we always need more to be happy.

We started to make our way back to our campsite, passing the tables and the girls again. I walked a few extra steps and then called to my kids, "Hey, guys, why don't you go on ahead to the campsite. I'll meet you there."

They looked at me with curious eyes, but the tone of my voice must've convinced them it was better to get out of there already.

I backtracked and walked over to the picnic table, setting my coffee down and swinging my leg over to sit down as if we were old friends. As if I had been invited. They looked at me and I looked at them, which alone almost gave me a contact hangover.

"So," I began, "I'm at the campsite right next to you."

And the look on their faces all but said, "Fuuuuuuuuuuuck meeeeeee."

I continued, "Look, I totally get it. I know this is going to make me sound like your mom, but I was in my twenties once."

Pause.

"The thing is, I fucking love swearing. I love it. You can't

imagine the level of control it takes for me to not swear in front
of my kids."

They looked uneasy.

"But my kids had to listen to you guys swear for hours last
night. HOURS. And they heard some swears I'm not even sure
I recognized. They are eight and ten years old, you guys. And
they had to listen to all of that shit. Again, I get it. I get having
a good time. But here's the thing—we also deserve to enjoy this
park. This is our weekend too. I've already complained to the
park ranger. We're not having another night like that."

They went on to tell me it was the guys who were the problem, that those same guys were leaving this morning, and they
were sorry. Not effusively, not like they owed me anything, but
more to save face. More to make me just stop talking and go away
already.

I rose, tipped my coffee to them and said, "Good. Have a
nice day." I smiled the whole way back to our campsite. If you
can't mess with someone twenty years younger than you while
they're having one of the worst hangovers of their lives, what are
you even doing?

As our campsite bustled back into activity—and the campsite next to us went about preparing breakfast in a silent even-
breathing-is-too-loud stupor, shooting us wary looks—we were
finally able to savor the best parts of this best-worst camping
trip. We saw sunrises and sunsets, one sunset in particular the
most stunning I had ever seen, right on the summer solstice. My
daughter waded around in the shallow water and I snapped a
photo of her, her silhouette sharp against the liquid orange light.
I laid down after lunch in an open stretch of grass on a soft cotton blanket and listened to the buzzing of bees, the fluttering of
bird wings so close. We had gathered pinecones and ferns, leaves
of all shapes and feathers and a smidge of a robin's eggshell. I

had taken in wildflowers bobbing back and forth in the breeze, we goose-stepped our way across rocks to go swimming, and we wolfed down Snickers ice cream bars at the campground store.

It was one camping trip that started horribly and turned into something greater than we could've imagined. We stuck it out and were rewarded, when typically I would've cut bait and left pissed off at the world.

Dad Camp is now a ritual that fills up arctic winter days with the promise of better, warmer days to come. Jon takes care of reserving the sites and paying for them, arranging who goes where, and beyond that, I don't know any details. Happily.

This past year he left with the kids only a couple of hours after they came home from their last day of school, summer vacation starting immediately. He told me later that when he drove into the park and checked in at the office, the park ranger looked over the sites he had reserved and said with caution in his voice, "Now, you know you're responsible for all of these sites, right? And for all of the behavior at these sites?"

As he told me this story we both laughed and I said, "Burton Island. That's what he was expecting."

That's when Jon explained that he understood, that this was actually the third year this big group had camped there. That it was a big group of dads and kids. That's when the ranger lit up and said, "Oh! It's you guys! We love you guys!"

Me too, park ranger. Me too.

Just Because You Can, Doesn't Mean You Should

I have come face-to-face with gratitude every single day since the heartbeat on the monitor decided to keep beating, every time it continued to beat. And those two times I went to the hospital and left with a fully alive and complete baby, and every single moment since.

I do not need to keep a journal to remind myself.

I am grateful for my children's lives, above all. I'm grateful they are not jerks, as far as I can tell. And I'm grateful they genuinely enjoy meeting and talking with our neighbors more than I do, therefore making them excellent spies.

I am grateful they were both born years before the invention of the iPhone and social media, so when I nursed them I had to occupy myself the old-fashioned way, by reading W and watching the Red Sox win their first World Series since 1918. I couldn't text or use emojis or e-mail while lightly resting my elbows on my baby's sleeping body. Instead, I paged through copies of *Vanity Fair*, stared into space, stared at his face and his jaw or her closed sleeping eyelids with those searching eyes underneath.

I am especially grateful none of that existed so when I was completely at my wits' end, I didn't also have to endure posts from other moms of their infants peacefully napping in cleanly designed cribs with modern color palettes and graphics. Or babies who were bright-eyed and bushy-tailed smiling—always smiling!—their gummy grins showing how happy they were to be alive. The best babies. That would've been fucking *it*, as I could barely shower or sleep or figure out what either of their problems were. I sweated through two summers with nonstop baby ragers covered in their own spit up. If social media had existed, the only thing I probably would've been able to post would've been, "Do you guys like my armpit hair? I've been growing it out."

I have wished for a lot of things over the years. I have wished for good health like the good getting-older person that I am. In my twenties I used to think "At least you have your health" was a polite way of saying "It's so sad you're so single and such a friggin' loser." I now know that wish is a good wish indeed.

I have wished for all good things for my kids, for them to be happy and safe, to be safe forever. I have wished for them to have cheerful lives and retain their good, tender hearts. I have hoped they find satisfaction and purpose in how they spend their days. If they spend their days ticking off dates on a calendar, just waiting for something to happen, it would fracture my heart in about three places. I hope they will return to me always, happy and healthy, wanting to see me, not out of some sense of duty or because it's a holiday. I have wished, more than anything, to have the kind of relationships with them I see and envy in others.

I hope they won't make fun of me behind my back or roll their eyes when I call them to say I love and miss them. I hope they will love and miss me back.

I have wished misery upon their enemies and a smaller amount of misery upon people who are just plain mean to them. There is a part of me that's counting on lightning bolts of regret shooting at will from my fingertips and straight into the jugulars of those who wrong them.

Pretty typical mom stuff.

I have maintained an identity for myself more or less since

the day my son was born. Less in those early hours and days and years, but then picking up with the speed and momentum of a runaway eighteen-wheeler ever since. I am building myself up at a breakneck speed and, to be honest, it feels fucking great. I wonder if I am leaving my family in my wake, but I don't want to stop. I have stopped so many other times.

I think about how old my kids are now, eleven and thirteen, and I almost can't say their ages aloud. It's as if their birthdays were a surprise this year, almost as if they don't happen every year on exactly the same dates. I'm not sure how I got here, yet the gratitude I feel at having made it this far is overwhelming.

I have spent years wishing for a bubble of personal space only to discover that twelve is apparently the age when kids stop holding your hand. My daughter isn't quite there yet. When we were in Maine this past summer I realized my son never reached for my hand. This vacation and that place was the one place that hand-holding was guaranteed, on our morning walks, us two early birds out for a stroll. I kept this in mind as my daughter and I walked to our joint haircut appointments the other afternoon. I stuck my hand out for her to grab and I immediately realized how long it had been, because the motion felt awkward and surprising instead of automatic, the way it used to. It felt electric. She immediately grabbed for it, perhaps thinking the same thing, in her own way. From the minute our hands clasped together, she started doing a skipping-sliding thing in her flip-flops, I think the joy she felt at holding hands was a big part of it. Her hair flowed and bounced behind her like a shampoo commercial. She felt safe and smaller and it filled us both with joy. We should hold hands every chance we get, while we still can.

I wish I could go back and talk to my new mother self and tell her all the things she should do differently. I would tell myself I shouldn't let anyone who hasn't had kids into our house in those first few weeks. That I will still feel the need to try to clean and do dishes and there just isn't time for that shit but I'll do it anyway. Then a friend who is not married and has no kids will breeze in with a gift and spend most of her time looking at me and wondering why I don't look happier. I will feel like I am going to explode; I will feel worse than I already felt and I already felt plenty bad. I will wonder if, in addition to losing myself (I won't know that's temporary yet), I have also lost all my single child-free friends. How could they ever understand what's happening to me? *I* won't even understand what's happening to me.

I should've made more friends immediately, as if I was a second grader. I shouldn't have been too proud or too shy to ask for walking dates or coffee dates where we could nurse side by side. I needed that. I should've asked for help sooner, even though I was raised to not ask for help, so it feels like the worst thing I could ever do. Even worse than asking for money.

Someone—anyone—should've told me to be alone with my husband more. It seems so obvious now, but I'm talking 2004 and 2006, and superhot takes and listicles for what new moms should and shouldn't do didn't really exist back then. Did they? Those were wildly different times and how stupid is that? Why does the world have to move along so fast? Maybe one day it will move in reverse and we will suddenly embrace taking long wagon rides across prairies and we'll write with quill pens and ink. Remember the calligraphy craze back in the 1980s? What was that about?

Back to the marriage thing. We lost each other. In a big way. And we waited too long to do anything about it. We thought that once we had a reliable babysitter and more money, we could make up for lost time. But a marriage is not a to-do list and you can't just catch up in a flurry.

I remember friends of ours—actually they were my husband's

friends first, I met them on our first date, then they became our joint collective friends. I remember a conversation with the wife after they divorced—even now I still can't quite believe they're divorced; they were so fun and great together; they were easy to spend time with; I genuinely liked (and like) both of them so much—and she said, "It was just so hard after the kids were born. You think it will come back one day. I remember thinking, *One day when the kids are grown we'll look back on this and laugh.* Instead, he told me he didn't love me anymore and wanted a divorce."

Sometimes you don't look back and laugh.

Sometimes you just get a divorce.

I wish I had heard that story before we had kids or maybe right when they were born. I needed to hear that earlier, I needed to hear it often. I'm not sure how much we can do about it all now. Maybe it's too late.

We each slept on the couch for months, trying to keep one or the other kid asleep. To say we were two ships passing in the night would be a disservice to ships passing in the night, which sounds downright sexy compared to what was actually happening. We would soundlessly pass one sleeping kid off to the other, or I would hand him a yowling baby with an angry, "I will throw this baby against the wall if someone doesn't get her away from me." We did all our sleeping and napping with kids on us at some point. We fed ourselves breakfast and read only the headlines from the front page of the paper, all while bouncing a bouncy seat with one foot. A one-man band. We swaddled and attachment parented the shit out of those kids and yet. Apparently we should've been doing some attachment marriage-ing as well.

Just because you can do something, just because you can push yourselves to the limit, just because you can work sixty hours or not take vacations or not go out to dinner with your partner or not even start the day with a hug and a kiss and a "Yeah, this is insane. But we've got this," doesn't mean you should.

Just because you can, doesn't mean you should. I have said this like a mantra ever since.

I wish I could be easier on myself, although the evidence clearly shows being hard on myself works. I do get what I want, mostly. I do not get things handed to me, although frankly it would be nice at this point. Like you know how celebrities get goody bags stuffed with La Mer and tennis bracelets at award shows? They already *have* money, and lots of it. No one should be giving them shit for free. But now? I'd like a piece of that action.

I wish I could have just one day of knowing what it would be like to walk around with a supermodel ass. It must be amazing. I wish there was something like that, like instead of fantasy baseball camp there could be fantasy supermodel-ass camp. I would go to that. I'd pay double.

I wish I could know what's going to happen next. But even if I had the opportunity to find out, even if someone could tell me, I would refuse. Even if they promised it would be great, I would be too nervous to find out.

I wish I could stop wishing. I wish I could just say thank you, this is enough. This is plenty. Look at me, being grateful.

LAST

You Are All the Joy

Allow me to embarrass you. No matter what you believe, I actually don't do this nearly enough.

You, both of you, are the soft hands that are getting rougher, from cartwheels and riding bikes, scrambling over rocks and grass like long-limbed crabs. Those hands have gone from stubby things that poke out of a mush of baby pudge to long, slender instruments. And although I keep thinking you must have the longest, most slender fingers on earth I realize that calling Guinness World Records over them is perhaps a step too far. Regardless, I admire them frequently. I never tell you that, because is it weird for your mother to admire your long fingers? I think it might be. But this is what we do.

You are the velvety, pillowiest cheeks. I have let my lips linger on those cheeks more than on any other cheeks before or since. And even though you are now eleven and thirteen you give me this much. You let me linger and kiss your cheeks. Not in front of your friends, I mean, you haven't lost your minds. But at bedtime I can still do that. I can also hold your head in my hands and make smooshy goldfish faces with your mouths or beep your nose and smooth your hair.

Your faces have meant more to me than any other faces because yours are the only faces on this earth I saw first. Even before that, I felt them inside me and honestly, how weird is that? It's getting weirder the more distant those days become and the taller you grow. Your faces were built inside my own body, an eyebrow from here and a nose from there; I'm not sure where those cheeks came from but I'm so happy they're here. Although in your faces I see traces and features from our family's past, I mostly just see you, in all your meandering weirdness and wide-open souls, your confusion and sadness, your fart jokes and naughtiness. Your love. I see the whole of you, as you are. And when I see your eyes well up, it hurts me more than if I was just crying myself. Seeing either of you sad is the saddest I ever feel.

You are the eyes that are the only eyes in existence to see how I actually am as a mother. So no matter what I write or post or tell other people, only you know the truth. I have failed you daily, I know. I have paid attention when you weren't interested and not paid attention when you begged for my undivided eyes and ears. I wish I could go back and do it all perfectly or even start from this square right here, but I can't. I have the best of intentions and then just let them fade, and now you are both at the ages where you call me out on it. "You said we would definitely do this today and I knew it wouldn't happen. I just knew it."

I don't want to wish that one day you will feel overwhelmed, that you will feel the tug between your own life and the lives of your children and the goals you set for yourself and how none of that fits neatly together. If it's a puzzle, it could only be the kind of puzzle that you get at a yard sale, a bag full of random pieces thrown together and good luck with that. But I hope eventually you will understand how I feel now, if only for a day, if only to know I was trying to do just enough to make it all work. Not do it all well and certainly not do it all flawlessly because obviously that's impossible. But to be all in on Team Good Enough. Maybe there is never such a thing as good enough when it's your own mother. Maybe the only way to know for sure is to have your own kids. It just seems with all our technology we should be able to leapfrog that a bit. Maybe a virtual reality "have kids" and "keep trying to live your own individual life" and "feel overwhelmed by all of that" experience could take the place of the home ec classes that are sporadically taught and still very much needed. The carrying around of a hard-boiled egg or a sack of flour bit doesn't even come close.

Your eyes are drawn from us, that much is clear. You with Dad's eyes and you with mine, sort of. They are big, beautiful eyes, perfectly suited to your faces. I almost can't take them in; they overwhelm me. Together, we have seen chapters upon chapters through those eyes. We have seen how unpredictable and scary a crowd can look even if, before you were born, that crowd would've looked fine to me. You have taught me how to see a bucket loader and an excavator because those are apparently two different things. And you have showed me the teeniest, tiniest flowers, the inchworms or neighborhood dogs or spotted piglets, and that I really shouldn't be worried about you when you jump from a crazy-high boulder into an untamed swimming hole. (I will still worry.)

We have been looking into each other's eyes since the first time you were each laid upon my chest and in my drugged-up trying-not-to-hyperventilate state—because as it turns out you get cold fast when you've been sliced open and you can't feel half your body and honestly was I really awake for that?—I remember those eyes. And each time I looked and saw those eyes I thought, "Of course." All those months of wondering what you would look like, of churning my imagination in an attempt to see all the possible faces, and of course when you were born you looked completely, exactly, and precisely just like . . . you. It was as if a part of me expected your faces, those eyes, all along.

You have filled up my days with spark and purpose. No

matter how much work there is to be done, I always feel a bit down when I'm staring at your backs as you leave to catch the school bus or when I see your sweet faces as you wave to me from the window as the bus rumbles by. And my heart floats when I hear the familiar sounds of the screen door swinging open, a backpack dropping to the floor, and sneakers or flip-flops or snow boots getting kicked off. Of course I tell you those things must be put away immediately and in the right places because we're not animals, but know my first emotion is gratitude that you are home. That you are with me. Again and again and again. I wonder how I will do when those sounds of doors opening and bags dropping are as infrequent as to require an actual holiday.

You are the ears, the *M*A*S*H*-era Radar ears that can't hear me tell you to turn the TV off but can hear sirens from across town. Yours are the ears that hear music, save it into the hard drive of your brain, and allow it to come out of your fingers when you sit down at the piano later and play it all back. Yours are the ears that we looked at suspiciously when you were a baby; you had that one small round bump right near the opening of your ear. Thirteen years later, it's still there. It has done nothing to harm you, and when I see it, just like your particular raised eyebrows, it reminds me you were once that small little baby who could fit neatly into the curve of my arm. Sometimes I crook my arm and trace an oval shape within it and say, "Baby Walker used to fit right here" and you always tell me to stop, but I know there is a part of you that loves it. It is the part we all have inside of us, it's the part that wants to remain small and cared for.

You fill up our house with sound; piano and the radio, "Mom, listen to this," as you read me something from your books whether I'm listening or not. There is a small Nerf basketball tossed into that hoop over your closet door and your mouse Oat's squeaky wheel that kicks in right around bedtime. There is giggling and fighting, hair drying and the loudest singing in the shower I have ever heard in my life. Sometimes it's overwhelming, all of these stations coming in on the same frequency, and I jam my middle fingers into my ears while I'm trying to draft an e-mail or just think a thought. So that first day of school after summer vacation? Although I have been waiting for it and I am ready, the silence almost breaks me. I can't believe it's only 9:45, 10:15, 11:30, noon.

I worry about what I will do with that silence when you both are grown. What will I do with that? Is it payback for me shushing you and waving my hands at you when I was on a work call in that NO-NO-NO-OH-MY-GOD-GO-AWAY way that I did? Is this the slow burn? I wish I could deposit those sounds in a bank, to take out when everything is too quiet, when I'm traveling away from home, when I'm down. I would withdraw the sounds of you both running down the beach in Maine under the moonlight with sparklers and I would withdraw you telling me the dream you had about a unicorn when you were three. I would withdraw you calling me "mama" because it's already been years since you've called me that, and I would withdraw every single time you unabashedly whispered to me that you love me, love me, will love me forever and will live with me always. I would withdraw every time you asked and begged for my attention, to look at a plane, a truck, a police car, a train, a ferry, a lobster boat, a snowplow, an excavator, a cement mixer, a helicopter, a tractor trailer truck, a car, an ambulance, a fire truck. You wanted my attention so much, all the time, and I didn't always give it to you.

I would withdraw the milk-drunk lip smacks and the kitty-cat cries; I would withdraw the sounds your mouth made when you were a toddler and you were talking and breathing through it constantly, huffy and puffy. I would withdraw all those and then some, to deposit back in my heart, to remind myself my life was full of sound and I cursed it. I wondered when I would have silence and time to think. I would remind myself this silence is what I thought I wanted.

You both hum. So did your great-grandmother. It's a trait I had completely forgotten about until I was in a thrift store one afternoon and heard the elderly lady who volunteered there humming away. A light and lilting da-da-dee-da-da-da as she arranged and rearranged. In this stranger, I heard my grandmother's voice again. And when you hum, I feel like you are having a conversation with her. It brings her close. I hope you never stop humming.

You are the metronome, the ticktock that has always been inside you. You hear rhythms in your head, you play them on the kitchen counter, the floor, you click-cluck them with your mouth. You used to get in trouble for that in class. They had to create "strategies" for you to stop. You are older now, and instead of strategies you have peers. They're the ones who comment now, about all those sounds you make. This has been described as "disruptive" in the past. It's taken me all this time to think, yeah, maybe disruptive *is* exactly what it is. You should always strive to be disruptive in this world. Fitting in and doing what is expected only leads us to be good, little, middle-of-the-road humans. Yuck.

You are the gentle heart and the scientist, the dreamer and the realist. Four years ago, one of the worst fights you got in that whole summer was over the fate of a cricket. There were so many crickets in our backyard; we heard them all summer, chirping to one another. One had become entangled in a spiderweb and Walker wanted to watch the spider eat the cricket. He understood the food chain and predators and prey. This was how life worked; this was how all life worked really. But Hawthorne wanted to save the cricket—the mere thought of sitting there and observing another creature being killed and eaten felt so morally wrong as to actually be insane. I raced from the house when I heard the explosion of shrieking, shouting and tears, surely someone had been hurt, a stick to the head, something. Instead, you stood in front of me with those big blue eyes, and tearfully explained that the cricket had just been leading its cricket life. It had not been bothering anyone; it was just going about his cricket business. You explained it deserved to be saved, it deserved to live. Just like we all deserved to live. What if its family was worried about him?

But by then it was too late for the cricket.

It was the angriest you've ever been with your brother. You felt utterly betrayed. It was as if you realized someone you loved with everything you had was, in reality, an actual monster. I understood both of your arguments; I was on both your sides. Most mothers are the worst kind of mothers, the non-side-takers. There are so many sides now. I used to think the world was like a box with a finite number of sides and angles, then you guys showed up, started growing up and disagreeing and branching out into the original and weird and lovely human beings you are and I came to accept instead that it's a faceted world, with infinite planes and endless reflections. I know each of you as well as I can ever hope to know anyone and so, I absorb your anguish. I understand your arguments and I want to be on your sides, both of you. But mostly, in those moments when all hell is breaking loose, I soften to the point of collapse when I realize there are still souls in this ugly world who care so very much about the fate of a cricket.

You were born a team. You will need to continuously search—with sincerity, with love, with good intentions—for the side you can both always be on. You have sharp minds and good hearts, so I trust you will be able to do this. Please do this for me. Historical evidence suggests it is possible, you've always had a connection others have commented on. You get along so well, you play together so well, you genuinely seem to *like* each other. That's what they'd say. Of course you are like all siblings and there are power struggles and tattling and smacking and betrayal. I understand everything is changing at a rapid pace for you right now. You're entering big, scary, exciting phases in your lives. But you still make each other laugh—hard—you understand each other so well that if we're in a bookstore you can each find a book the other might enjoy (and you'll be right), and you love each other with everything you've got. Most important, you have each other's backs. I hope you always, always will. Long after your father and I are gone.

You are all the change I feel in my own life, the change I'm not sure I'm ready for. But here it comes, ready or not.

The other day, Walker wanted to play a game you guys had invented when you were little. Walker is obsessed with trucks. Hawthorne is obsessed with animals. And the game you invented is called Tranimal Day. Granted, the naming could use some work. Mostly it consists of animals riding around in trucks, pretty straightforward as games go. You have played it for years. And you would play it for hours; sometimes it could easily take up half the day. I always thought of that game as the ultimate expression of your connection, of you understanding what makes the other tick while also getting exactly what you wanted for yourselves. I felt proud of that game in the typical way parents feel proud of something they had exactly nothing to do with.

You have played this game less frequently over the years, and it's not like I expected you to come home from college and play it or anything, but when Walker wanted to play it this past week and you said no, you didn't want to play that game anymore, you just weren't into it anymore, it was for little kids, it was silly, well . . . I'm pretty sure both my heart and Walker's heart broke at the exact same time. I think I even said something in a slightly desperate tone like, "Are you sure?! Oh, you should play it. You used to love that game!" when really what I wanted to say is, "How can you be outgrowing things like this, silly things, things I hadn't thought about but which suddenly mean the world to me, without at least giving me a heads-up? How can you go about this business of getting older without so much as a second thought when I am at least on my thirty-ninth thought about it? I'm not ready, why are you ready?"

I've spent so much time thinking about your firsts, I haven't thought so much about your lasts. It's hard for me to imagine you'll never play that game together again, not even once. But this is the process, I guess. Such a stupid process.

You are the ghosts. I see you in strangers and strange scenarios, in new landscapes you've never seen and in people you've never met. I find you. I see your arched brow or your giggle. I see the things you love and they make me think of you. You were with me when I saw horses crowded along the fence line of a pasture in Oregon and I went three miles out of my way to turn around and go back. I couldn't just keep driving away from those horses. I knew you would love to see a picture of them. You are with me when I'm on a plane and as I'm getting close to landing at a bigger airport than ours back in Vermont, I peek down and see the FedEx hangar with all those planes gathered around like piglets at their mama's teats. I think about how almost every morning when I used to drive you to school when you were little, we'd see that one single FedEx plane coming in for a landing every morning at 7:35. The regularity of it was comforting, like an alarm clock confirming we were already awake and on our way.

One time I saw a youth choir perform at a Christmas party and there was a boy singing who was probably three years older than you. He was the teenage you, right down to the glasses and body type. I felt like I was standing twelve feet away from the future you, and I slowly sipped my glass of wine and tried not to cry. I see you everywhere.

You are with me wherever I go.

You are everything I didn't know I needed—in the many specific and unexpected ways I've come to need you—and now I cannot imagine the arc of my life without you. You have already forgiven me a thousand times over and loved me through my faults and impatience, my grouchiness and bad cooking.

You are all the joy I can hold and, gratefully, more than can sometimes be contained. I can feel you both growing away from me and, of course, that's how this thing works. So when you hold my hand or let me touch your hair, I notice. Randomly and oddly enough, I often think of what Blythe Danner said during her portrait session with her daughter, Gwyneth Paltrow. Annie Leibovitz relayed her words. She had said she "really hadn't been able to hold her daughter like that since she was a little girl."

I read that quote years before I would become a mother and I have never forgotten it. Some part of me knew already, how close we would be and then how we would necessarily move away from one another. I realize now I have already held you as closely and tightly and freely as I ever will. That all of that is already over. It hardly seems fair. It hardly seems like enough. It wasn't enough. And now here we are, with each spin around the sun you move further away from me until, one day, you are loose in the world and our fingers and arms no longer touch.

You weren't born to be children always, always mine. You were born to be people, out in the world. I can't hold both of you to me until the end of time; it's unfair to all of us. What exactly would the point of that be anyway? And I can't hold your hands all along the way; your hands must be free and open to hold other hands. Your friends and lovers, your own children maybe one day.

You are all the joy this life has brought me, in two original packages. I've attempted to pour into you what I've learned but I know that will only get you so far. You will need to do and see, feel and hear. You will need to make mistakes, big and small. You will need to feel the utter insult of other people's carelessness and callousness. You will need to understand that people you love and trust more than they deserve will go on to break your heart. Honestly, I'm still trying to understand that myself.

You are all the joy I hope to absorb and observe, love and learn from in the years and decades to come. I have given myself over to you both in ways you will never know. And that's okay. That's what mothers do. I hope you will fall in love—with yourselves, with your lives, with only the people who truly deserve you. And I am beyond words and thoughts and thank-yous that you are mine.

My perfectly imperfect children.

When I Die

When I die, hug each other with force, until no one wants to be the first to let go. I let go first a lot. I can tell you now, I regret it.

Look into each other's eyes, and pretend I am looking into them too. Sometimes I had trouble with that. Know that I was lucky and loved far beyond what I deserved. Know that I loved you. Or as my friend Dave Spancer—who is already dead—once said, "I love you all. You're amazing. Except for the few of you who suck, but even you have your endearing qualities."

If my children are still quite young when I die, do not tell them to honor me with forced smiles, this is no Celebration of Life. Not yet. Do not ask them to mind their manners, to say "Thank you" when someone says, "We're so sorry about your mother." Life has betrayed them.

Let them lie down on the ground and kick and scream. Let them rage like wild animals, gnashing their teeth at the unfairness. Let them retreat and close up like a morning glory after the sun has gone down. It's what we all want to do when someone we love dies anyway.

And wait. Do not plan a funeral or any other thing that would take away from what they need. Circle the motherfucking wagons. Be there for them. Surround them relentlessly with love. Make Mother's Day something they won't dread for the rest of their lives. I don't know how you'll do it, but do it. Take them to the beach on my birthday and listen to the waves, watch the seagulls grift and swoop. Read books with them and tell them, "There were so many more books she wanted to read." Read all those books.

Talk to them about the things that are happening now that you thought I would've liked very much. Tell them I loved them; I will love them always. Tell them that I'm so sorry I left them. What kind of mother does that? The worst kind, the kind made from flesh and blood and bone.

When they are ready, when they feel like they could dance and laugh and do the same party tricks with coins that they did at their great-grandmother's wake, throw me a party. A big one but nothing too expensive. The previously alive me loved an open bar and a reason to dress up. Do those two things. I don't care if you serve food, as many of you know I couldn't feed myself at parties to save my life. So to speak. If you want to truly replicate how I lived, serve mac and cheese at 2:00 a.m. and make everyone eat it straight from the pan.

If you toast me, whatever you do, raise your glass with a "Here's looking up your old address!" Henry Blake delivered this toast and the only way it could've been better is if Hawkeye delivered it instead. But beggars can't be choosers, especially beggars who are dead.

Tell stories about me, but don't humiliate me. I lived my whole life in fear of humiliation. What you thought of as snobbery or shyness or a reluctance to play volleyball? I just didn't want to be embarrassed. So don't embarrass me. I might be dead, but I feel confident this particular fear will live on.

I cared very much how I looked in photos. But I'm dead now, so I guess you can choose the photos that you like. I have no more opinions to give. Choose the photos that show how you remember me and how you'll think of me. Show my kids who I was apart from the person who nagged them to clip their wolfen toenails and lost her temper over the most petty nonsense.

Assuming I haven't been smashed by a giant boulder or burned to a crisp, wash my body, if you can, if you can get through it. If I ever took care of you, please take care of me this one last time. Please don't let a stranger do it. It's just a body; don't be scared. It loved and lost, it nourished and disappointed. You'll see that my dead-person skin isn't so different from your alive-person skin and these arms and hands that stiffen are still the same. They do not turn to scales, they are not the arms of a swamp monster. You always said I had cold hands and, well, at least this part should be consistent.

Kiss my forehead one more time. I don't know what it's like to be dead but I would bet my earthly possessions (that are all yours now anyway) that forehead kisses still register.

Clip my hair, save its strands. You might not want them now; you might not want them later. But somewhere down the road I have faith that a descendant will marvel at her great-great-great grandmother's brown-gray hair and realize that it's so very much like his or her own. We are a brown-hair family, full stop.

If, in between tears, you are not making inappropriate jokes, then how can you claim to have ever loved me? What's wrong with you? Get out. I mean it.

Just kidding. See?

When I die, throw me by the fistfuls into the ocean. I prefer the unforgiving slate-gray waters of Maine, but it's not a deal breaker. It will matter more to you than it will to me. My ashes, like ghostly silt, will cling to your fingertips and float on the surface of the water. You might mistake this for my reluctance to leave, but I am already gone.

Maybe give some of my ashes to my enemies. It'll bring

them joy knowing I'm gone for good. They can do something petty like flush me down the toilet. *Dicks.*

I worried a lot when I was alive. So when I die, take comfort that I'm no longer worrying about these things:

Am I a good enough mother?

Am I good enough, period?

Why can't I be more generous with people who love me?

Am I crazy? Like crazy-crazy?

Are my kids okay?

Will my kids always be okay?

I wonder if I just have regular dandruff or it's some kind of serious skin condition that I can't seem to ask a doctor about ever?

Should I have wanted a bigger family?

Should I have been such a whore in my twenties?

Should I have been more of a whore in my twenties?

Who the president is.

What's wrong with the world.

What's wrong with you.

What's wrong with me.

What's wrong with everybody.

How I'm going to die.

When I'm going to die.

I can't believe I'm going to die.

I'm no longer worrying about anything.

I'm no longer here.

Where has the feeling gone?

The show must go on.

Acknowledgments

Sometimes you will be told (or will tell yourself) that you are not smart. And sometimes you will be told (or tell yourself) that you are not funny. You will become a mother and tell yourself that you're terrible at this, you can't believe it's this hard, why didn't anyone say anything, how can everyone not see that you have no idea what you're doing? Why are brainy people like doctors leaving tiny vulnerable human beings in your care? Don't they know? It is so easy to not believe in yourself, especially as a girl, as a woman, always. Thank you to anyone and everyone, friends and family and strangers, who saw in me things I couldn't see in myself.

Thank you, Scot Armstrong, for sending me that random Facebook message about my costume for that Halloween-in-August party, which turned into my asking for your advice about a screenplay, which turned into my coming to LA for that dinner at Chateau Marmont—where I was the only lady eating fries and drinking beer—which turned into my accidentally raking a glob of cheese across my lap and having to walk everywhere with my purse clutched in front of my thighs, which inexplicably turned into you still cheering me on and telling me, after my first *McSweeney's* acceptance, to forget about a screenplay for now and write a book of short pieces with this: "Right now you are the Ramones. Keep being the Ramones. Don't switch to jazz on Thursdays." You are the best person.

The most sincere this-book-would-not-exist-without-you thank-you to Chris Monks, editor of *McSweeney's Internet Tendency*. Thank you for that first acceptance and every acceptance since but especially and forever for saying "I like this one" to "Please Don't Get Murdered at School Today." It was not a ha-ha piece. It was a piece I wish didn't have a reason to exist at all. And it wouldn't have had a natural home anywhere else. But there it was. And that's where Ryan Harbage read it and sent me the nicest e-mail I had ever received about my writing while also suggesting maybe he would like to be my agent. Well, that was an excellent afternoon. Thank you for being the most responsive and respectful editor anywhere, but mostly thank you for not being a twentysomething hipster. You do our people proud.

Ryan Harbage, thank you for that e-mail (which I will save forever), for your many kind words of encouragement since, for wanting to vomit all over Trump as much as I do, for your excellent taste in GIFs, but most of all for finding such a great home for this weird-ass mental breakdown of a book.

Profound thank-yous for saving my bacon to crack investigators, stellar insiders, and "Let me explain this to you as if you are a small child" great friends Rachel Livsey and Jeff Leeson. I owe you both.

Stephanie Hitchcock, I'm really sorry you had to edit this book while you were pregnant. I thought the joke was on me when I had to write the entire thing during my kids' summer vacation, but I now think the joke was on both of us. Sorry for writing things that made you cry (but not too sorry). Thank you for confirming for me, through chatty "AND THEN GET THIS THING MY HUSBAND DID" or "WHAT ABOUT WHEN THIS HAPPENS AT WORK" conversations, that you were always the right and only editor for this thing.

A very special thank you to poet and neighbor, Julie Cadwallader Staub, for permission to excerpt her wonderful poem and to designer Joanne O'Neill for the most perfect visual metaphor married to a Wes Anderson-y cover I could ever ask for.

Major high fives or long uncomfortable hugs (whichever you prefer) to the generous friends who encouraged me as I started to share my work. Those early votes of confidence meant more than you know. Thank you, Aimee Boulanger, Kate Barnes, Eric Olsen, Winky Lewis, Teresa Elliott, David Doyle, Cindy Cagle, Erik Shonstrom, John Siddle, Vanessa Violette, Emily Blistein, Marie Claire Johnson, Nicci Micco, and those I will remember I forgot after this is printed. Special thanks to weekend design heroes Michael Dabbs, Jen and Byron O'Neill, and Allison Ross. Y'all know why.

This book wouldn't remotely be in its current form and would contain a lot more *goddamns* if not for my readers Laura Haines, Darren Higgins, Beth Urdang, Charlotte Moore, and Tanja Alger. For five parents with summer vacations, actual jobs, pressing social media obligations, and/or eclipse-viewing road trips to deal with, you crammed a lot of reading and note-taking into a stupidly short period of time and I can never thank you enough. On my knees and bowing down with special gratitude for Tanja, who offered to restructure this book for me and then actually *DID*. Please rescue other people's books for a living.

I am incredibly fortunate to have been raised in a family of independent, trail blazing, and lipstick-loving women. Judy Harrington, Janet Masse, and Theresa Masse—thank you for populating our family tree with unapologetic greatness. I wish Mary Arrow was alive to see this book, partly because she thought *freelance* was just a fancy word for *unemployed*, but mostly because she never missed an opportunity to show me she loved me, and this book represents all my love in return.

Thank you, Paul Harrington, for my laugh, my sense of

humor, for Maine, and for never telling me I couldn't do something because I was a girl. Also thank you for teaching me how to throw a punch. It's my favorite.

I wouldn't have been able to write this book at all without the selfless support of my husband, Jon Hughes, who not only helped make the children I write about but also whisked them away for camping trips and day trips and basically raised them motherless during the summer of 2017. Thank you for trusting me and believing in me even though I'm crazier than a rat in a coffee can. You didn't ask me to change a word of this book, allowing me to be honest and raw about things that are Not Fun. We both know that if the tables were turned, I wouldn't be nearly as generous. So, *thank you. I love you. I'm sorry.* Let's party.

Last, given this is not only a book about motherhood and children, but also about being a woman, living in this country, right now or ever, at this particular age or at any age, I would be remiss if I didn't say a profound and heartfelt thank you to the hot-ass chicks who are the main reason I'm surviving any of this shit. To Amanda Gustafson, Meg Rupert, and Jen O'Neill, no one is better than you. And no, no one ever told us it'd be this hard.

About the Author

KIMBERLY HARRINGTON is a regular contributor to *McSweeney's Internet Tendency*, the co-founder and editor of parenting humor site *Razed*, and a copywriter and creative director. Her work has appeared in *The New Yorker*, *Timothy McSweeney's Quarterly Concern*, and on *Medium*. She lives in Vermont on purpose.